D0060662

businessbuddies

successful coaching & mentoring

For further success in all aspects of business, be sure to read these other businessbuddies books:

Successful Assertive Management
Successful Communication
Successful Conflict Resolution
Success in Dealing with Difficult People
Successful Decision Making
Successful Finance for Managers
Successful Interviews
Successful Leadership Skills
Successful Negotiating
Successful Performance Reviews
Successful Strategies for Growth
Successful Time Management

businessbuddies

successful coaching & mentoring

Ken Lawson, M.A., Ed.M.

BARRON'S

First edition for the United States, its territories and dependencies, and Canada
published 2007 by Barron's Educational Series, Inc.

Conceived and created by
Axis Publishing Limited
8c Accommodation Road
London NW11 8ED
www.axispublishing.co.uk

Creative Director: Siân Keogh
Editorial Director: Anne Yelland
Design: Sean Keogh, Simon de Lotz
Consulting Editor: Ken Lawson
Production: Jo Ryan

© 2007 Axis Publishing Limited

All rights reserved. No part of this book may be reproduced in any form, by photostat, microfilm, xerography, or any other means, or incorporated into any retrieval system, electronic or mechanical, without the written permission of the copyright owner.

NOTE: The opinions and advice expressed in this book are intended as a guide only. The publisher and author accept no responsibility for any loss sustained as a result of using this book.

All inquiries should be addressed to:
Barron's Educational Series, Inc.
250 Wireless Boulevard
Hauppauge, New York 11788
www.barronseduc.com

Library of Congress Control No: 2006932161

ISBN-13: 978-0-7641-3703-7
ISBN-10: 0-7641-3703-4

Printed and bound in China
9 8 7 6 5 4 3 2 1

contents

Introduction

You're finally holding a responsible position as a manager. And just when you think you've jumped the highest hurdle in your career story to date, you're staring upward at another one, even higher and more challenging than the others: How to succeed in your job as well as you can, and how to manage and motivate others to do the same.

Managers do not work alone. As the title implies, they have responsibility for overseeing projects and people. But how do managers learn the principles of management? How do they develop the skills they need to guide their colleagues and reports? How do they tap into the potential that will maximize their own job performance and that of others?

The key that unlocks the answers to these questions is the process of professional development. Responsible managers—indeed all career-minded professionals—need to be lifelong learners. They need to continually develop new skills and competencies, and let go of old, outmoded ones. And, they need to develop increasingly complex approaches to collaboration and organizational effort.

Successful Coaching & Mentoring provides managers with the tools they need to foster the developmental process that will produce peak performance in the workplace. As a manager, you'll learn how to identify areas of need and how to prioritize them. You'll learn the differences between developmental and remedial coaching, and gain clarity about the benefits and realities of each. And, you'll understand the differences between coaching and mentoring.

Chapter 1 introduces a scenario that might very well reflect your own professional situation: How does a new manager recognize coaching and mentoring needs, and pursue strategies to implement meaningful developmental programs? You'll read about the

Introduction continued

similarities and disparities of these two kinds of professional relationships and learn about the types of developmental need that call for one or the other. You'll also get acquainted with the types of people involved in the process: coaches, mentors, and beneficiaries.

In Chapter 2, you'll read about the potential obstacles to the coaching and mentoring processes—the restraining forces that could impede their success in developing the potential of coachees and protégés. You'll learn how to anticipate these roadblocks and drive around them as you move forward with meaningful coaching and mentoring.

Chapters 3 and 4 focus on the many benefits of coaching and mentoring for a new manager—and his or her colleagues and reports. You'll learn why developmental programs provide positive outcomes to the professionals at both ends of the relationship—and, in very tangible ways, to the organizations that sponsor and encourage them.

The last chapters describe the nuts and bolts of both processes in clear, comprehensible language. You'll learn exactly what goes into a successful coaching or mentoring program, how each unfolds, and what is reasonable to expect each type to accomplish.

Successful Coaching & Mentoring offers valuable guidance for managers who are dedicated to success. In straightforward, reader-friendly language, it portrays professional development as a prerequisite for peak performance, organizational benefit, and career success. Whatever your position, this guide will provide a wealth of useful insights, tips, and strategies. It's a true sourcebook for lifelong learners.

Ken Lawson, M.A., Ed.M.
Career Management Consultant
New York

1

what are coaching & mentoring?

Coaching defined

OVERVIEW

Coaching and mentoring are time-honored practices in the workplace, but their function as management tools has grown dramatically in recent years for three main reasons:

- the end of the traditional "job for life" security
- the lack of formal apprenticeship programs
- the rise of a performance-led culture of employment

This first chapter:

- outlines the the main definitions of both coaching and mentoring
- highlights the main similarities and differences between them
- describes some of the characteristics of those people who coach and mentor
- outlines the types of employees who can benefit from coaching and mentoring

WHAT IS A COACH?

The term "coach" is most typically used in a sports context to refer to an individual who is hired to encourage an individual or a team to improve his or her performance. The effectiveness of a coach is usually measurable in the short or medium term by these concrete results—improved times, more wins, fewer losses, and so on.

Although this sporting analogy translates well into a business environment, there is one major difference. Company results can't only be measured by a straightforward win/lose scenario. A company may win many battles over a year while losing out in other important areas. Even if the company posts negative results, the changes in a way of working or composition of the workforce may yield improved results in two or more years' time.

What coaching is deceptively like

Coaching can be easily confused with these other ways of developing people:

1

TEACHING

Although the best teaching is interactive, encouraging students to think for themselves, the role of the teacher is mainly active. The teacher instructs and tutors from a set curriculum that the pupil has to absorb and learn mostly, until the latter stages of school, without questioning. Coaching is also instructive, but a coach does not merely prescribe ready solutions. He is there to encourage the individual or team to take a far more active role and to work out for themselves how to make the best of their abilities.

2

COUNSELING
Counseling also aims at improving performance but by digging up often painful and uncomfortable personal issues that are not necessarily linked with work and the workplace. Coaching is not aimed at such long-term and personal intervention in any way.

3

MENTORING
This is the term most commonly confused with coaching, and although they share many similarities, coaching and mentoring have fundamental differences. This book aims to explore the many contrasts between them. For a quick overview, see pp. 28–31.

Basic features of coaching

The following list covers the main functions of coaching:

1

TO SET GOALS

As in sports, a business coach has to start by establishing what the person or people want to achieve in the short, medium, and long term. Without clear goals, it is difficult to decide on a strategy.

2

TO EXAMINE TACTICS

Also similar to a sports coach, the person steering a business team has to outline the different options open to reaching the goals. This doesn't mean the coach makes the final decision on what tactics are to be used. He can give advice, but the ultimate decision has to come from the individual who is receiving help.

3 TO SET TARGETS

As a way of seeing if the tactics chosen are working, coaching helps to establish small targets to measure whether a strategy is broadly successful. Like the decision on tactics, the coachee should have the final word on the nature and number of targets that are set.

4 TO CHALLENGE ASSUMPTIONS

If there are certain rules in the business, the coach should make sure the individual or team is aware of them. But rules are also to be broken. Coaching is aimed at questioning working practices, even when the same ones have been followed for a long time.

Basic features of coaching continued

5

TO POINT OUT WEAKNESSES

The coach is not providing a proper service if he skirts from uncomfortable truths. Identifying a coachee's weaker points and signaling ways of improving these to minimize their negative effects on overall performance is one major responsibility of a coach.

6

TO MAXIMIZE STRENGTHS

As well as being aware of negative behavior or work patterns that need to be modified, a coach should also accentuate the strengths of each candidate so that the candidate can make the most of his abilities.

7

TO PROVIDE FEEDBACK

A regular review of progress is vital to make sure the appropriate strategy has been followed, to know when significant improvements have been made, and to give employees encouragement and praise to keep developing.

8

TO PROVIDE FOCUS

Coaching is generally a short-term activity with the exception of executive coaching (p. 35) where a longer time frame is necessary. It also tends to concentrate on specific work-related issues. Therefore, it provides focus on a specific issue.

Mentoring defined

WHAT IS A MENTOR?

A mentor is typically an older individual with a wealth of experience who chooses or is chosen to help and guide another individual who is normally younger and, more importantly, far less experienced. The onus to be a role model is far greater for a mentor than for a coach.

WHEN IS A MENTOR NEEDED?

Mentors typically work in businesses such as law firms where trained but inexperienced staff benefit from the knowledge that senior staff have built-up through years of practice.

ORIGINS OF MENTORING

The word "mentor" originates from a character from Greek mythology. When the King of Ithaca, Odysseus, went to fight the Trojan War, he entrusted his household to his old friend Mentor. In particular, he asked Mentor to serve as teacher and overseer to his son, Telemachus.

WHAT IS A PROTÉGÉ?

Also known as a mentee, the term protégé refers to the less experienced person who is receiving and benefiting from the acquired wisdom and years of practice of the more experienced individual.

What mentoring is deceptively like

Mentoring can be confused with these other ways of developing people.

1

TEACHING

There are many elements of teaching in mentoring, such as the emphasis on passing on knowledge. However, the frequency and flow of information is established equally between mentor and mentee. As mentoring is not a private lesson, the mentor requires far more effort and initiative from the protégé than a teacher expects from a student.

2

COUNSELING

Mentoring seems closer to counseling than coaching because mentoring takes a broader view of a protégé's concerns, rather than a narrow focus on a particular aspect of a job. The longer-term nature of the mentoring relationship also requires, like counseling, that both sides establish an open and trusting relationship. However, mentoring in the business world is still focused on career issues, rather than personal ones. In addition, both participants are intended to benefit in different ways from the relationship. In contrast, a counselor's job is to focus exclusively on the "patient." In order to create a trusting relationship, the mentor needs to stress confidentiality and show respect for the mentee.

3

SPONSORING

Mentors are like sponsors in the sense that they create opportunities for the protégé that would not normally be open for them. However, sponsors have tangible reasons for helping a mentee such as raising the mentee's profile and demanding certain results within a given time frame. A mentor's support for a mentee is more altruistic, and normally far less self-serving. Most mentors believe they are giving back something to the business community,

4

COACHING

There are many characteristics common to both coaching and mentoring, which is why both terms are often used interchangeably. This is an error. However, there are some basic differences between the two approaches. These are spelled out on pp. 28–31.

Basic features of mentoring

The following list covers the main roles of mentoring. Notice how many share similarities with coaching.

1

TO DEVELOP SKILLS

One of the key purposes of coaching and mentoring is to help employees find out more about their ambitions and to hone their skills to the best effect to achieve these goals.

2

TO PLAN FUTURE

Both coaching and mentoring are geared to produce future results, to predict future scenarios, and to look at the different options available to get there.

3 TO ENCOURAGE ACCOUNTABILITY

Unlike sports coaches who are hired to drum in techniques and strategies at their protégés, business coaches can't dictate the way employees must perform unless they are at a very junior level. Athletes strive for a narrow focus, but business leaders must be able to adapt to circumstances constantly and to change strategies accordingly. They have to learn to think for themselves, not following others footprints or beliefs. Mentors are doing their protégés a disservice by laying down rules and ways of doing things. They should be drawing employees out as much as possible. Both coaches and mentors are there to encourage protégés to become self-reliant and independent.

Basic features of mentoring continued

4

TO SHARE, NOT INSTRUCT

It is important to stress that mentoring is not "telling" the less experienced people how to deal with difficult situations. Nor is it about delivering a template or a set of rules for handling awkward situations. It is laying out their own experiences and skills as well as providing a context so that protégés can tackle future difficult situations for themselves.

5

TO PROVIDE A ROLE MODEL

More often than not, mentors are chosen for their past accomplishments and the way they have pulled through difficult struggles. They lead by example and, in the case of mentors who are still working, through the ways they handle present problems, which the protégé can observe.

6 TO FOCUS ON GOALS

By acting as a sounding board for protégés, mentors listen and ask probing questions about short- and long-term objectives and ambitions, not just in their current employment but in their careers. Because mentors are not anxious about the delivery of immediate results, they have more time to encourage their protégés to focus on their ultimate goals.

7 TO SUPPORT

For somconc starting out in the business world, no matter how talented or promising, corporate life can be bewildering. A mentor is there to offer a measure of support.

Coaching vs. mentoring

1

COACHING FOCUS
The focus is primarily on how to improve issues at work or specific aspects of the job.

MENTORING FOCUS
The emphasis is on long-term career. Any discussion of the current job is put into a wider context of future ambitions that are not restricted to the present company or job.

2

COACHING TIME FRAME
There is typically a fixed period set for the relationship. Once the problem has been resolved, or the skills passed on, the contract comes to an end.

MENTORING TIME FRAME
The duration of the relationship is more fluid because the targets are more long term. There is no specific end point to the relationship.

3

COACHING SCHEDULING
The narrow focus of the issue and the time restrictions means that meetings are normally carefully structured. They also tend to be scheduled at regular intervals.

MENTORING SCHEDULING
The flexibility of goals and issues at stake are reflected in the informality of meetings. There is greater scope for spontaneity in the meetings.

4

COACHING
AGE AND EXPERIENCE
The coach does not necessarily have to be an expert in the subject she is coaching. Nor does she have to be much more senior in either age or overall experience.

MENTORING
AGE AND EXPERIENCE
Mentors are mainly chosen for their expertise and knowledge in a given field. Inevitably, this means that the mentor will be far more qualified than the protégé.

Coaching vs. mentoring continued

5

COACHING AGENDA
The need to achieve immediate, specific goals sets the agenda. The objectives are often set by management, not by the employee.

MENTORING AGENDA
The agenda is looser because it looks to long-term gains. The mentee sets the agenda.

6

COACHING
FORCED OR VOLUNTARY?
Coaches are often forced upon employees, especially if the coach's responsibility is to raise the performance of an entire team.

MENTORING
FORCED OR VOLUNTARY?
Employees specifically seek out mentors. It is crucial that protégés are actively receptive to guidance.

7

COACHING PAYMENT
Many coaches, if they are external, receive a fee and teach staff new skills, or work to improve a particular situation.

MENTORING PAYMENT
Mentors almost always provide protégés with advice and guidance out of goodwill and out of duty and gratitude, to spread what they have learned through the generous nature and intervention of others.

Types of coaching

Coaching is available in many forms and is paid for either by the employer, which is the most typical scenario in big companies, or by an individual in the case of a small business.

1

TEAM COACHING

As in sports, a business team produces the best results when all the members are working toward a similar goal and agree with the methods and approaches required to achieve their targets. Team coaching focuses on creating a shared vision and working collaboratively.

2

PERFORMANCE COACHING

As the title suggests, this type of coaching focuses on improving performance and can be applied either to an individual or to a team.

3

SKILLS COACHING

This type of coaching has a much narrower focus. A certain set of skills has been identified as lacking or not up to stanadard as part of an earlier round of more general coaching.

4

CAREER COACHING

Career coaching focuses on an individual's concerns about how to develop his career. Unlike mentoring, with which it shares many characteristics, it can be restricted to a few sessions aimed at providing general pointers.

Types of coaching continued

5

BUSINESS COACHING

The onus with business coaching is less on the needs and ambitions of an individual and more on the objectives of a particular business or company.

6

LIFE COACHING

Life coaching, as the name suggests, encompasses all aspects of an individual's life. Although it is not strictly limited to workplace issues, personal ambitions and frustrations do spill out into business life, and for that reason, it is included in this section. The most relevant questions asked by a life coach to business include: "Why am I always late for deadlines?"; "What is really motivating me at work?"; "What other job would I like to be doing if I had a choice?" and "What would I like to be doing in five years' time?"

7

EXECUTIVE COACHING

This "one-on-one" focus on generally the most senior personnel is becoming increasingly popular. Training managers more often than not involves external coaches or consultants.

8

DISTANCE COACHING

This type of coaching refers more to the methods used to coach rather than the specific type of training involved. Distance coaching describes coaching received at a distance, whether via the telephone, e-mail, instant messaging, or video conferencing. Distance coaching can be applied to an individual or a group.

Types of mentoring

THERE ARE THREE BASIC TYPES OF MENTORING RELATIONSHIPS:

1

FORMAL MENTORING

Formal mentoring is fostered by companies that deliberately assign senior managers or directors to oversee a certain individual who they think will most benefit from guidance. This is the modern-day equivalent of an apprenticeship, which was so common a hundred years ago but which faced considerable strains in the more fast-paced and competitive environment of businesses today. However, as the high popularity of TV shows such as *The Apprentice* reveal, young, enthusiastic people who are starting out in business crave the wisdom and experience of a senior individual who has their interests at heart. This is particularly the case in today's business environment where employees change companies and even professions frequently. There are fewer available senior personnel with the time and commitment to share their experience.

Formal mentoring is also referred to as "planned" mentoring because it has literally been devised and arranged by the company. The formality of the arrangement may mean that mentor and mentee restrict the relationship to the office and to the company. This contrasts with informal mentoring.

2

INFORMAL MENTORING

Informal mentoring matches an experienced individual with an inexperienced person. These cases cover experienced individuals who like passing on their knowledge and single out a few individuals who they think will be receptive and inexperienced employees who make a point of seeking out a senior colleague for advice. As this type of mentoring is not enforced by the company, both mentor and protégé have to be committed to the process and enjoy the collaboration. As long as the relationship lasts, the two members must believe they are not being forced in each other's company and they need to take each other's time seriously. These relationships don't necessarily have to be formed within the same company or even the same sector. It is not unusual for informal mentoring to take place in a company where formal mentoring is also encouraged. They can co-exist quite happily.

3

SELF-MENTORING

Calling for high levels of motivation and self-discipline, self-mentoring requires mentees to develop their careers through self-tutoring tasks and courses and through extensive networking. It is most successful when the person has already been mentored before or is highly aware of the best ways to approach mentoring.

Who coaches?

There are two main types of coaches. Most companies use a mixture of both.

INTERNAL COACHES.

A growing number of managers are being encouraged to act as coaches for their staff, in spite of the reluctance by some to see training and development of employees as anything other than peripheral to the activity of focusing on achieving tangible results for the company.

Apart from senior managers, internal coaches can also be colleagues, peers, line managers, or members of the human resources department.

WHEN IS IT BEST TO USE THEM?

1 When you need coaching to happen urgently. Hiring external experts can be time-consuming during a crisis.

2 When you want to cut costs. Consultants can be expensive. Ask yourself whether some of your managers are qualified to do the same job.

3 When it's necessary for the coach to have a clear understanding of the company's culture and politics.

4 When you want to build a high level of personal trust over a long time. This is more likely when you have a director inside the company.

Who coaches? continued

EXTERNAL COACHES

These coaches are often specially trained to impart information about developing people skills and may even be used to contribute in training managers to become more effective coaches.

WHEN IS IT BEST TO USE THEM?

1 When the issue that needs to be improved in the company is very specific and there is no senior member of staff with the requisite expertise. Hiring a professional to coach one or more managers ensures that the skills that are needed are brought into the company.

2 When the information you need to introduce is rather sensitive and you anticipate a heated response from employees. An outsider may not face such a critical response, or will be able to respond to criticism more objectively.

3 When senior managers are too busy firefighting and the time they spend coaching would be better used attending to critical operational matters.

Who mentors?

Because mentoring can be both formal and informal, so the types of mentors and their qualifications can vary widely. These are some of the most common types of mentors.

1

FRIENDS AND FAMILY

These represent the most informal mentoring relationships, but they still need to demonstrate commitment and consistency on both sides. Particularly in the case of relatives where there can be histories of personal conflict, these relationships need to strive for as much objectivity as possible and not bring unrelated topics into the main discussion. The focus of any discussion should be about developing a career path. WIth a friend as mentor, care must be taken to keep the relationship balanced: a friend must not think her time and expertise are being taken for granted.

2 SENIOR PERSONNEL

Directors within your company that you seek out don't necessarily have to be at the most senior levels but they should have considerably more experience of business life than you do. The most beneficial mentors will be the ones the protégé admires for a particular achievement or style of working because the motivation to listen and learn from them will be that much higher.

3 DIRECTORS IN YOUR SECTOR

If protégés find discussing their future careers with direct bosses too sensitive, then a common option is to refer to senior directors in rival companies. Clearly, in this scenario, confidentiality might become an issue so there must be a high level of trust on all sides.

Who mentors? continued

4

DIRECTORS IN OTHER SECTORS

Often, directors who work in a completely different sector can provide as much insight and advice in your career as someone inside your sector. The principles of goal-setting, listening, and asking questions remain the same.

5

INDUSTRY ANALYSTS, CONSULTANTS

Though many mentors are happy to impart their knowledge and experience for free, there is a growing industry of analysts and consultants who will impart useful information and guidance for a fee.

6 RETIRED EXECUTIVES (SCORE)

The Service Corps of Retired Executives offers entrepreneurs free mentoring and workshops at hundreds of local offices across the United States. The service provides an online database of their mentors who can be contacted via e-mail.

7 PROFESSIONAL ASSOCIATIONS

Professional associations or trade bodies within your sector are likely to offer some sort of mentoring program.

Who needs coaching?

Most people in the workplace receive some sort of coaching during their careers even if it is only for a limited time. Everyone stands to benefit from effective coaching in core and more advanced skills at different times. The most common recipients of coaching tend to be junior and middle managers. The following are situations where coaching is typically valuable.

1

SHORTAGE OF TALENT

When companies are facing a skills shortage for whatever reasons, they may be better off developing the skills of current employees through coaching sessions than on recruiting external candidates. This is a more cost-effective option in the long term, although the cost of hiring in a coach can be a high "one-off" expense.

2

STARTING UP A BUSINESS

When a small group of people start a company, they may find they are doing several jobs at once and are not particularly qualified for some of them. A few coaching sessions on some basic skills can help.

3

STRUCTURAL CHANGES

When a company is being merged with another or during a period of massive layoffs, there will be some staff expected to cover new areas of expertise for which they are not prepared. Coaching can help them to gain a better understanding of these roles.

Who needs coaching? continued

4

NEW RECRUITS

Whether they are graduates or higher level executives, new arrivals in a company usually benefit from a short period of specific coaching on certain skills and tasks. All companies work differently, and new recruits need to be told how this particular company works.

5

FAST TRACKERS

Although it is difficult to show favoritism in the workplace, there are inevitably going to be certain middle managers who are being singled out for fast track promotion. These managers may require extra coaching so they can keep up with fast-rising careers.

6

SENIOR EXECUTIVES

Even the oldest and most experienced directors in a company benefit from coaching, particularly if they have earmarked areas of expertise that they feel they are lacking.

7

POOR PERFORMERS

Before blaming poor performance or disappointing results on employees, managers should look critically at the support the company has given them and whether performance could have been improved with more coaching and training.

8

USERS OF NEW TECHNOLOGY

Rapidly changing computing and telecommunication systems mean that employees must be coached on a regular basis on how to make the most of the new technology.

Who needs mentoring?

Most workers would benefit from the care, consideration, and attention to detail that formal or informal mentoring can provide for career development.

However, a list of the types of employees and working situations that most commonly demonstrate an urgent need for mentoring follows.

1

NEW COMPANY HIRES

By virtue of being newcomers to a company, new hires are always high on the list of workers who stand to benefit from a mentor, even if this is only for a settling-in period of between three to six months. “Showing the ropes” to new hires helps them to hit the ground running, producing their best work in the shortest time.

2 NEW DEPARTMENTAL HIRES

These candidates may already have worked in the company for some time but have been transferred to a new department or division and would benefit from being shown the ropes in their new area.

3 HIGH POTENTIAL EMPLOYEES

Inevitably even in companies who strive to provide all employees with equal opportunities, there are going to be certain candidates who stand out from the pack. These employees are believed to have high potential for rapid promotion, so senior management will want to mentor them to make sure they fulfill their potential. The expectation is that through mentoring, their needs and aspirations will be catered to within the company to prevent them from being poached by a competitor.

Who needs mentoring? continued

4

LOW-ACHIEVING EMPLOYEES

Employees who are not performing to the best of their abilities are also candidates for some mentoring. This is particularly the case when managers perceive that these employees have potential and that they are hard workers but that their efforts are not yielding results. Mentoring can help them find out what is stopping them from reaching their potential. Even with more problematic candidates who are less willing to improve their performance, some mentoring may be easier than dismissing them to avoid any legal battles and to save costs on future recruitment, which could be avoided.

5

PEOPLE ON CAREER BREAKS

With career breaks becoming more common as people strive to balance work interests with life goals, there is a need to ensure that people coming back to a company, after six months to a year away, fit in smoothly again and are brought up to speed on new developments. This also applies to women and men who have taken time away from the workplace to stay home raising their babies and small children.

6

MOTIVATED STAFF

There are a small group of employees who may not necessarily have been pinpointed as future leaders of the company but who are nevertheless ambitious to improve. These individuals may request a mentor by their own initiative.

The new manager

WHO IS HE?

A "new" manager is a prime candidate for both coaching and mentoring. He is typically a highly effective worker who is promoted within the company thanks to his technical expertise and his potential for leadership.

CASE STUDY

Brad Turner has been appointed as director of sales at a multinational hotel in a major business destination. For the last three years, as sales executive, Brad has garnered an impressive track record for sales of:

- rooms to visiting businessmen and women
- conference and meeting spaces for local and regional companies
- catering/dining gatherings for companies

HIS NEW CHALLENGE?

Brad's job is to lead a team of executives, most of whom were doing his same job just a month ago, to create an annual budget and ensure the team sticks to it; and to monitor that customers are satisfied with the product.

COACHING NEEDS

HOW TO SET TARGETS

In the last three years, Brad's primary concern has been to reach his sales objectives according to targets set by the former director of sales. Now he has to set the targets, not only for himself but for the whole team.

HOW TO BUDGET

Until now, Brad never had to worry about the size of the company budget unless it directly affected the amount he was able to spend on expenses or on the sales target of the month. As the new manager, he must create an annual budget and track it monthly. For this, he will have to liaise closely with the finance department.

HOW TO PROMOTE THE COMPANY
As a sales executive, Brad was an excellent communicator of the benefits of the hotel over the competition. In his new capacity, he will no longer be able to rely on his own efforts to promote the hotel. He needs to oversee an official strategy that involves marketing, advertising, and special promotions.

MENTORING NEEDS

TO SHOW LEADERSHIP QUALITIES
While skills such as working out budgets and masterminding a publicity campaign are skills that Brad can, in principle, learn after a few designated sessions, working on leadership issues is a more complex and long-term challenge that demands a patient and persistent guide.

TO HANDLE DIFFICULT PEOPLE
As a self-starter with a cheerful, positive attitude, Brad has never found it difficult to motivate himself to improve his performance. As manager he has to motivate others and that can be difficult when it may no longer be appropriate to maintain the same level of friendly informality with former colleagues. Some workers will be difficult to handle. To deal with complex interpersonal relations, Brad is best served referring to regular advice from an experienced and trusted mentor.

Checklist: When to coach/mentor

WHAT SITUATIONS ARE MOST RELEVANT TO COACHING?

1. DOWNSIZING When a company is laying off workers, the employees who remain may have to take on new responsibilities. ☐

2. SPECIAL ASSIGNMENTS When a worker is given a special project or assignment, this could demand learning new skills. ☐

3. NEW PRODUCT/SERVICE LAUNCH When a company is launching a new service or product, employees may require coaching to understand it and pass information on to clients. ☐

4. PERFORMANCE REVIEW During a review, skills a worker needs to acquire or to develop must be identified. ☐

5. INDUSTRY-WIDE CHANGE When new technology is introduced, workers have to catch up quickly. ☐

WHAT SITUATIONS ARE MOST RELEVANT TO MENTORING?

1 STARTING OUT Steering is particularly important for interns or trainees so that both employee and employer maximize the beginner's raw talents. ☐

2 RETURNING AFTER LONG ABSENCE When employees return to a company after pregnancy, illness, or study leave, they need guidance on current practices in today's fast-moving world. ☐

3 DOUBTING DIRECTION When a person is having doubts, it can help to talk to a trusted mentor in confidence. ☐

4 CHANGING DIRECTION When a person has decided what course of action to take, it is good to seek advice from an experienced mentor outside the company. ☐

5 ASSUMING A SENIOR POST A new senior manager may need advice on assignments, expectations, and leadership skills. ☐

CHECKLIST

2

obstacles to coaching & mentoring

Corporate obstacles

This chapter outlines the three main obstacles to the formal practice of coaching and mentoring in the workplace. It is vital to understand these sources of resistance to be able to overcome them. They are

1. Corporate barriers to the benefits of coaching
2. A manager's own prejudices and mistrust about coaching
3. Other employees/colleagues' skepticism of coaching

OBSTACLES BY THE COMPANY

The following are the most typical reasons why companies fight the need to devote time and resources to coaching and mentoring.

1

LACK OF TIME

By far the most prevailing reason given by companies for not embarking on coaching are encapsulated in the phrases "no time" or "not the right time." Ironically, if senior management or the main decision-makers in the company are too busy firefighting to pay attention to coaching, it means there are some fundamental time management problems in the company that need to be tackled. Coaching people to use their time more effectively could reverse this chaotic pattern of behavior.

2

LACK OF RESOURCES

Competing with time restrictions as factors for not coaching or mentoring is lack of funds. However, a company that has not budgeted for any of the mid- to long-term benefits of coaching for the sake of obtaining some short-term gains, may find that it is missing opportunities of improving revenue flows.

Corporate obstacles continued

3

LACK OF UNDERSTANDING

When the exact benefits of coaching a team or focusing on an individual are misunderstood, then it is difficult to persuade senior executives to embark on activities that are not linked with the core business of the company. Coaching must be seen as a fundamental part of a manager's responsibilities, occupying a main role in the company rather than a tacked-on duty or pastime.

4

INERTIA

When a company has chugged along for several years with no coaching or mentoring practices in place, old ways of doing things become deeply entrenched. People dislike having new ways of looking at their business through a mixture of laziness and fear of how changes may affect their roles in the company.

5

AUTOCRATIC TENDENCIES

Although vertical structures are less prevalent in big companies than they were two or three decades ago, there are still many organizations, even smaller businesses, that have a defined group of leaders who insist on stamping their own ways of doing things on the rest of the staff. Coaching in these scenarios, because it brings directors and employees together, can be viewed by some managers as a threat.

6

FEAR OF ASKING QUESTIONS

Companies that are run in more traditional, paternalistic lines can also resist coaching practices because these imply that there may be something wrong with existing methods and raise questions of past decisions. Directors of these kinds of businesses may also think that if they hired the appropriate staff, then these people won't need any further training or tutoring.

A manager's own obstacles

When a company shows resistance to introducing formal coaching structures, it's not surprising that managers adopt these same prejudices. These are some of the most common reasons why managers distrust coaching and mentoring.

1

EXTRA RESPONSIBILITY

Unless managers are themselves sold on the benefits of coaching, they may assume that having to implement a coaching program will eat into their own time without reaping immediate benefits on their resources. They can also begrudge having to take on extra responsibilities that are not part of their formal job description. Providing direction and assessing where employees need to change working patterns is integral to a manager's role, not an additional activity.

2

LACK OF EXPERIENCE

Typically, managers resistant to coaching have themselves never received any formal coaching so they can think they don't have the background and know-how either to coach staff themselves or go about finding appropriate coaches.

3

LACK OF SUPPORT

As outlined in the "corporate obstacles" section, working within a company culture that does not encourage coaching and mentoring makes it doubly difficult to introduce these practices. The manager is fighting two battles at once—persuading employees of the benefits for themselves and, at the same time, getting the support of senior management for the introduction of these practices.

A manager's own obstacles continued

4

FEAR OF STAFF RESISTANCE

Even managers who can see the benefits of coaching for their staff may anticipate widespread antipathy to the practice by employees. They may assume that if subordinates or colleagues haven't asked for extra training or guidance, then they don't need it. However, it is a manager's responsibility to provide direction and to be aware of areas in which staff need to improve.

5

HANDS-OFF APPROACH

Managers who are self-starters and are clear about their goals can wrongly assume that other staff have the same capacity for initiative. It is precisely when bosses don't provide much guidance that staff not receiving much direct supervision will most benefit from coaching.

6 FEAR OF LOSS OF CONTROL

Some managers can be wary of coaching and mentoring. These managers fear that subordinates will grasp the opportunity of closer contact on self-development issues to air their grievances about their jobs and perhaps about their managers' management style.

7 LACK OF CONFIDENCE

Managers may be excellent at strategic thinking or at achieving concrete results (such as growth of sales or revenue) but still lack confidence in their personal skills. They might perceive coaching as exposing their inadequacy in dealing with other people.

Staff obstacles

Colleagues and subordinates have their own set of reasons for resisting coaching and mentoring. These include the following:

1

LACK OF GOALS

Employees will find it very hard to buy into the idea of taking time out of their already busy schedules to be coached in specific tasks unless they can see for themselves how this activity will help them in the long run. To understand the values of coaching, they need some sort of goal, or objective, however incidental or trivial.

2

LACK OF ROLE MODELS

Employees who are being encouraged to improve certain aspects of their work will only truly respond if they can see that senior management is making any necessary adjustments. Otherwise, any time spent on coaching will be ultimately seen as a time-wasting activity.

3

LACK OF TIME

Assuming that employees are persuaded that time devoted to being coached will be beneficial, they need to feel that management is taking into account their schedules. Without acknowledging these time constraints, management can make little progress with coaching sessions. Employees need to believe they have the right to attend these coaching periods without worrying about not carrying out other activities that would normally be completed during these times. Managers need to show their staff that they have made contingency plans (such as hiring a temporary worker or changing a deadline) to accommodate them during coaching sessions.

Staff obstacles continued

4

FEAR OF EXPOSURE

Just as managers fear that questions raised during coaching sessions can undermine their authority or way of doing things, so employees may be wary of how coaching sessions could serve to highlight any of their deficiencies or weaknesses. It is the responsibility of the manager or coach in charge of training or tutoring to underline that any coaching is available to help people to improve, not to find fault.

5

LACK OF COMMUNICATION

Employees who don't feel senior management is listening to their needs will also be typically resistant to any coaching because they will resent time spent on activities that are not relevant to their concerns. Managers need to listen and evaluate their personnel's concerns before imposing any coaching. The best way is to tailor any coaching or mentoring to what their employees want to get out of these sessions. This means actively listening to them and asking the right questions to get the right answers.

6

LACK OF INITIATIVE

Staff who are overly dependent on their managers to carry out activities and reach targets are ripe for coaching. Their lack of initiative may stem from various sources including lack of self-confidence, laziness, and lack of encouragement. The idea of coaching can be frightening to these individuals because they are being forced to make decisions and to come up with their own solutions.

7

PEER PRESSURE

Change is always unsettling, both in large companies and in smaller businesses. Individuals who respond positively to new ideas and new suggestions about their work may encounter pressure from more skeptical colleagues who aren't interested in changing their ways and, possibly, fear that they stand to lose by change.

Checklist: Identifying obstacles

To introduce the act of coaching and mentoring, you have to identify your biggest obstacles. Answer "yes" or "no" to the following questions to find out how aware you are of these barriers.

1. Do you know what your company's attitude is regarding devoting time to coaching? ☐

2. Does your company have a budget for coaching and mentoring? ☐

3. Are there successful examples of coaching practices in your company that you could use as a model for skeptical staff? ☐

4. Do you feel confident about talking about the benefits of coaching to your senior management? ☐

5. Do you feel capable of identifying areas in your business where coaching would be most beneficial? ☐

6 Are you aware of your colleagues' attitudes to coaching? ☐

7 Do you listen to people's concerns about self-development? ☐

8 Can you think of ways to juggle activities at work that will open up more time for coaching sessions? ☐

9 Are you able to communicate the benefits of certain coaching sessions to your subordinates? ☐

10 Do you invite suggestions about current working practices? ☐

11 Do you trust your staff and invite initiative? ☐

12 Do you like shaking things up at work? ☐

3

benefits of coaching

Benefits for the company

1

IN-HOUSE TRAINING

The majority of coaching is done in-house and even if carried out by consultants, it takes place in the workplace. This avoids the disruptions and inconvenience caused by staff being away to attend courses. It also means that coaches can use real working situations to try out any new techniques.

2

IMPROVED RESULTS

The better prepared a workforce is and the happier they feel with their own personal development, the greater the chances that they will perform to their full potential and achieve greater results for the company.

3

MONEY-SAVING

Effective coaching not only can yield better results, but it can also help staff discover where they may be wasting too much time on unprofitable activities or iron out obstacles that are standing in the way of improved results. The bottom line can be significantly affected by a carefully targeted coaching program.

4

SOFT INTRODUCTION TO CHANGES

Constant change is part of today's business environment, yet many employees find it difficult to navigate through uncharted waters. Coaching, however, can provide some assurance during difficult times by preparing staff for change. If coaching takes place well before any major changes, then it gives staff sufficient time to work through many of the typical reactions—denial, resistance, rejection, and acceptance—that take place during a period of, for example, downsizing or expansion.

Benefits for the company continued

5

ISOLATION AT THE TOP

Senior executives can feel isolated and unsupported when they are the ones making sure the rest of the staff are nurtured. Executive coaching, geared specifically toward top directors, can provide them with a sounding board where they can explore some of their thoughts and fears.

6

FOR RISING STARS

Inevitably, there will always be certain employees who are rising through the ranks faster than others and to prepare them for early promotion or new challenges, a period of intense coaching may be necessary. It also shows that the company appreciates and is keen to develop these high fliers.

7

FOR TECHNICALLY SKILLED

There are also many specialists in a company who need to be aware of any technological developments, and they are likely to require more periods of coaching in new systems than the average employee.

8

FOR IMPROVERS

There are also those employees in the company who may not be achieving their potential or, in the worst-case scenarios, are simply not pulling their weight. A period of coaching can help them identify why they are failing to produce the results expected of them and what they have to do in order to improve their performance.

Benefits for managers

The following are common advantages of coaching for managers, many of whom will be acting as coaches.

1

IMPROVED PERFORMANCE
Effective coaching is aimed at bringing out the best in managers. Being a better leader can result in a more committed and productive workforce and further improvements in performance.

2

BETTER RELATIONSHIPS
By understanding more about their own roles as coaches as well as their own roles as directors, leaders can learn to improve relations with colleagues and subordinates.

3

IMPROVED TIME MANGEMENT

Coaching can help a manager identify what tasks and responsibilities could be passed on to the most responsible and able employees. Delegating work can free up time for other urgent or core activities.

4

MORE CREATIVITY

By challenging established working practices, coaching can also unleash creativity in the workplace. Coaches encourage managers to experiment with ideas, to think outside the box, and to talk through any potential changes with senior management.

Benefits for managers continued

5

BETTER USE OF PEOPLE

Many managers may be good at their particular job but are blind to some of the experience and potential of their employees. Through coaching, they can develop leadership skills that make them more aware of their employees' skills and expertise.

6

ABILITY TO ADAPT TO CHANGE

Flexibility and adaptability to change are necessary requisites in a fast-evolving workplace, and coaching can help managers become more responsive to change and to make and implement the right decisions in a timely fashion.

7

POSITIVE WORK CULTURE

A workforce that believes their needs and objectives are being considered is more likely to be satisfied at work, creating a positive work environment.

8

STAR PERSONNEL

The highest achievers will always end up seeking promotion, if not within the company then elsewhere, but you can try to stave off their moment of departure if you provide coaching opportunities that are tailored to their needs.

9

UNPRODUCTIVE WORKERS

There are inevitably going to be some troublemakers in an office, or at least some candidates who are not reaching their potential. A manager's responsibility is to get the best out of his or her workforce, and coaching can present one way of motivating these workers to improve their performance.

Benefits for new managers

New managers (such as Brad Turner, see pp. 54–55), in particular, benefit hugely from receiving coaching on the following four skills:

1

HOW TO CONTROL FINANCES

Controlling the finances of a department or unit is one of the crucial tasks of a new manager like Brad Turner, but it is likely that he has never before been directly involved with the process. The finance department or the accountancy team can impart basic information, through a series of coaching sessions, on the following fundamental aspects of finance: accountancy rules, balance sheets, cash flow statements, and income statements. The most important skill for Brad will be how to set an annual budget and how to monitor it during the year, knowing that monthly targets are likely to fluctuate.

2

HOW TO MANAGE A PROJECT

Brad may feel under pressure to show both his superiors and his subordinates that he is doing something, or he may be too busy firefighting to set time aside to plan a project. However, managing a project effectively is one of the most useful skills Brad can learn. New managers who underestimate the importance of a plan, can find themselves reacting too late to a change in the market or an aggressive move by a competitor. Those who plan are far more proactive. A project forces them to concentrate on what is important.

3

HOW TO MAKE DECISIONS

Decision making is not a skill that a manager necessarily has by instinct. It is a skill that can be taught by senior managers with greater experience on making decisions. Brad can be taught how to define a problem or set of problems more carefully. He can also be shown the different techniques generally available for coming up with alternative solutions to a problem such as pareto analysis, six thinking hats, and decision trees. Finally, he can be shown the importance of selling the final decision to the team to make sure that the decision is actually carried out.

4

HOW TO COMMUNICATE

A new manager like Brad may have the best ideas and intentions in the world but if he is unable to communicate these to his colleagues and subordinates, these have little chance of succeeding. A coaching session on effective communication can help a manager to communicate clearly with his team. Skills covered include: how to listen; how to exchange ideas, feelings, and values; how to decide what information to relay and in what order; how to use nonverbal signals to emphasize messages; and how to provide feedback.

Benefits for coachees

Employees and coachees—the individuals receiving coaching—can enjoy several benefits from coaching.

1

PERSONALLY TAILORED PROGRAM

Coaching can be flexible and tailored specifically to an individual's needs and preferred learning style.

2

EASY DELIVERY

Coaching can also be planned around an individual's schedule and can be incorporated into an employee's schedule for times when he will be most receptive to the challenge.

3

FOCUS ON REAL WORK PROBLEMS

Unlike many development courses that can be too general or not focused on real working problems, a coaching program can concentrate on an individual's real work situation. The coach can help the employee develop solutions.

4 TIME SAVING

Instead of having to attend seminars or conferences on general topics, the learning possible through coaching can take place in the everyday office environment, saving an employee with a heavy work schedule considerable time.

5 A CHANGE IN BEHAVIOR

Coaching helps individuals look at their work patterns and evaluate how effective they are being. The coaching process can highlight areas that require attention and, possibly, areas in which a change in behavior and working methods and patterns is needed.

Benefits for coachees continued

6

GOAL-SETTING

Coaching forces employees to consider what they really want to do and to find out what tasks they must complete to achieve their objectives. Even if employees can't think of definite goals or at least not long-term ones, the process of introspection and analysis offered by coaching can at least point them in one direction.

7

BETTER DECISION MAKING

The ability to make good decisions is often about developing a clear focus, and this singlemindedness can often be provided by coaching.

8

RECOGNITION

Some employees may think they have been neglected by supervisors or some of their peers, and coaching can help to highlight their achievements and make them feel recognized.

9

COURAGE

Coaching can help identify an employee's strengths and give a worker the courage to seek out more challenging and responsible work. This benefits the individual's own development and also the company who can eventually promote the employee to a more senior role instead of spending money on recruiting new staff.

10

MORE BALANCED LIFE

Coaching encourages employees to delve into their professional goals and to see how compatible these will be with their personal goals. The end results can be that they manage to achieve a better work/life balance, which will ultimately benefit performance at work.

Checklist: Do we need coaching?

If you check the majority of these boxes, your company willl benefit from setting up a coaching program.

1. We do not have potential coaches on site. ☐
2. We need to improve our results. ☐
3. We have staff spending too much time on unprofitable tasks. ☐
4. We are planning big changes. ☐

5 We have several senior executives who have indicated that they feel unsupported. ☐

6 We have several young people with the ability to go far. ☐

7 We are operating in a high-technology sector. ☐

8 We have several people who are currently underperforming. ☐

4

benefits of mentoring

Benefits for companies

This chapter outlines the main benefits of mentoring to companies, managers, mentors, and mentees.

1

TO RAISE PRODUCTIVITY

Improving staff's understanding of their roles and unleashing their potential through mentoring can help staff improve their performance which translates into greater productivity.

2

TO ENSURE CONTINUITY

Because managers move from job to job more often, there is also less potential in companies for senior directors to pass on all their valuable experiences in the company to younger staff. Mentoring can provide an opportunity to pass on values, ethics, and standards. More companies are implementing formal mentoring programs to ensure this handover of knowledge takes place.

3

TO MANAGE CHANGE

Change of management styles, personnel, and company culture are more frequent today in an increasingly competitive market where mergers and acquisitions are common. Guiding personnel during these difficult periods ensures as smooth a passage as possible and prepares them to be flexible during a transition period.

4

TO INTEGRATE NEW RECRUITS

Mentoring is also beneficial for new employees who need special guidance and direction in their first few months at a new job. Managers save time and money in the long run with careful supervision of new recruits.

Benefits for companies continued

5

TO RETAIN QUALIFIED EMPLOYEES

The fast trackers are likely to be tempted by new opportunities, but mentoring them to help them acquire new skills or expand their horizons within the company can encourage them to stay on because they feel appreciated and their needs are being indulged.

6

TO DEVELOP LEADERSHIP STYLE

More managers are seeing the benefits of training staff to help productivity at work but also to develop their leadership skills. The practice of mentoring involves developing people's skills through example and guided practice. Mentoring raises the skills bar across the company.

7

TO UNDERSTAND STAFF

By mentoring junior staff, managers obtain a greater understanding of the challenges facing those working in the lower levels of the company.

8

TO INSTILL LOYALTY

Companies that organize mentoring relationships, or at least encourage staff to seek them out, are being proactive about their staff development, and this promotes a strong sense of loyalty and satisfaction.

9

TO CORRECT DEFICIENCIES

Mentoring can highlight any gaping holes in employees' knowledge and skills and attempt to rectify these deficiencies, which would otherwise remain unnoticed.

Benefits for mentors

Although there are major elements of generosity and selflessness in mentors' relations with protégés, it is too simplistic to characterize them as merely one-sided. Certainly, senior directors who have reached the top of their careers, may not make any professional or material gains by guiding an inexperienced individual. But there are a number of valuable benefits to the relationships. In fact, if mentors don't derive positive feelings from mentoring, the process would end fairly rapidly. These are some of the main benefits for mentors.

1

DERIVE PERSONAL SATISFACTION

There is considerable pleasure in seeing a promising talent blossom under a mentorship, particularly when the mentor has contributed indirectly to many of the decisions made on career paths and goals.

2

MAKE SENSE OF PAST EVENTS

By working on current challenges by using past and often difficult experiences, a mentor is forced to reflect on previous performances and to understand more about past events and decisions.

3

GAIN INSIGHT INTO PRESENT

For older managers who spend a lot of time with their peers (the majority in the same generation) and outside the main office, it is a refreshing and often enlightening experience to gain an insight into the day to day lives of younger workers. Finding out more about new practices and technologies, which they are not up to speed on because of their other senior responsibilities, may also help them make better managers in the future.

Benefits for mentors continued

4

GIVE SOMETHING BACK

Mentoring younger people can give busy professionals at the peaks of their careers a rare opportunity to give something back to the industry or business that has given them so much.

5

MAKE NEW FRIENDS

Just as the mentee finds that many doors open professionally through an effective mentoring experience, so a mentor has a chance of making new friends and acquaintances and undergoing new experiences.

6

IMPROVE SELF-IMAGE

The best mentors are greatly admired and respected for their vision and competence, and this can only further enhance a mentor's self-image.

7

ACHIEVE PUBLIC RECOGNITION

Even more senior directors who have achieved a lot need recognition, and they may not be receiving praise so often from their peers because everyone expects them to perform well. Mentoring, however, offers younger people a chance to respect and admire their mentors.

8

HELP SELF

The old adage that those who help others help themselves is very apt for a mentor because there are many positive outcomes from guiding others successfully, such as a sense of pride.

Benefits for mentees

Employees and protégés—mentees—have a lot to gain from a mentoring relationship. The gains include the following:

1

DEVELOPING OWN CAREER
With the end of "job for life" security and an increasing number of career changes, people have to learn to become more adept at managing their own careers. Mentors, both within the company and in different sectors, can provide a wide range of advice and expertise. A self-starting attitude is important to seek out the right mentors.

2

BUILDING CONFIDENCE
One of the main responsibilities of the mentor is to raise a mentee's self-esteem and to push her to tackle assignments that are beyond her typical remit or experience.

3

LEARNING BY EXAMPLE

Mentoring provides the protégé with a role model and sounding board, enabling him to develop new skills and approaches to challenges. In the best mentoring relationships, many different approaches to problems are discussed and options considered and narrowed down. Approaches that may be new to mentor or mentee can benefit both in the long run.

4

INTEGRATING EFFECTIVELY

For a young graduate or a new employee who has made a recent career move, mentoring enables a smoother transition into the workforce. A mentor can help inexperienced workers grapple with any unrealistic expectations they had of the company and the sector.

Benefits for mentees continued

5

EXPANDING OPPORTUNITIES FOR WOMEN, MINORITIES

Although the rights of women and minorities have grown significantly at work in the last decade, these groups still perceive they can be hampered by a lack of networking opportunities. Mentoring attempts to fill these perceived gaps in some companies by acknowledging that people of different genders and different backgrounds may need a different approach to their careers.

6

TACKLING CHALLENGING WORK

Mentoring means that employees can be taught or encouraged to attempt more challenging and interesting work. They do so because mentors work on their self-esteem and instill confidence to try new things out.

7

ENCOURAGING WORK FROM HOME

Technological advances have made work from home possible. For managers to trust and ensure that employees working from home can work as efficiently as in the office, mentoring is necessary, not just for the initial training but as a way of maintaining communication with the head office.

8

COMPLEMENTING STUDY/THEORY

Learning from the experience of others complements ongoing formal study and training.

9

DEVELOPING NEW NETWORKS

By having access to a new range of potential contacts made available by the mentor, the protégé has the possibility of opening doors that she didn't know existed and of widening her perspectives.

Benefits for new managers

New managers such as Brad Turner (see pp. 54–55 and 84–85) benefit hugely from receiving mentoring on the following three skills.

1

HOW TO IDENTIFY A LEADERSHIP STYLE

There is no one best leadership style. A new manager like Brad will adopt a style with which he is most comfortable. It is likely that Brad won't find out what his leadership style is until he has been fulfilling his new role for some months. Even though it is up to him to choose the style that suits him best, a mentor can help him by alerting him to some real case studies, either in the company or from past experiences. For instance, does a certain manager like to make his own decisions or does he like to bounce off ideas with other colleagues? Does another manager tend to stick rigidly to his strategy, no matter how circumstances change or should he be flexible and admit that an original plan of action needs to be modified? Which is more effective?

2

HOW TO DELEGATE

Most new managers have invariably been highly effective in one particular role, in Brad's case, at selling hotel rooms or banquet events to companies. However, now he finds himself having to accomplish several roles at once. It is impossible, given the list of new responsibilities and the limited time available, to be equally effective in all areas. It is vital to learn to delegate to other team members. But as an inexperienced manager, Brad may find it difficult to do this because he fears losing control. A mentor can help him become more confident about delegating tasks by encouraging him to part with certain functions, to choose who to delegate additional responsibilities to, and how to monitor the progress of delegated tasks.

3

HOW TO MOTIVATE OTHERS

As a sales executive, Brad was a classic self-starter who was highly motivated to keep on improving his sales record. As a new manager, the onus is now to motivate others. This isn't always easy because not all team members respond to challenges and targets in the same way. Brad may learn this through bitter experience and trial and error, but a mentor can help him prepare for these moments by encouraging him to examine what makes different people tick, by alerting him to the negative ways of motivating others (for instance, through unnecessary aggression), by rewarding good behavior, and by asking questions.

Checklist: Do we need mentoring?

If you check the majority of these boxes, your company might benefit from a formal mentoring program, or from encouraging your employees to seek informal mentoring.

1. We need to raise productivity. ☐
2. We want to keep the skills and knowledge we have in-house, regardless of personnel changes. ☐
3. The company is in a period of rapid change. ☐
4. We are taking on several new recruits. ☐
5. We have fast-tracked our potential high achievers and do not want to lose them. ☐

6 We want to develop our employees' leadership potential across the board. ☐

7 It's possible that our senior managers are out of touch with the realities of life at the junior end of the company. ☐

8 We want to encourage company loyalty. ☐

9 We want to be sure the company is operating at maximum efficiency. ☐

5

coaching in action

Assessing the coachee

This chapter looks at the main responsibilities of coaching. It begins with a description of the four main coaching stages.

1. Assessing the coachee
2. Establishing ground rules of the coaching session
3. Putting coaching skills into action
4. Reviewing results

COACHEE ASSESSMENT

Determine whether the coaching is developmental, for example, an employee has requested a specific type of coaching, or remedial, for example, the manager or the employee have identified certain areas that an employee needs coaching on to improve skills level and performance. The first stage is that the manager must thoroughly assess the coachee's current skills and ways of working. There are several steps to take in order to do this efficiently and effectively.

1

DIRECT OBSERVATION

As a manager you will try to pay particular attention to the employee's working patterns for at least a week and jot down your observations. Try to be as objective as possible and do not allow other people's perceptions to cloud your way of looking at current working practices.

Assessing coachee continued

2

ANALYZE RESULTS

Look at any quantifiable way of assessing the coachee's work. If in sales for instance, has the person reached or exceeded sales targets? If in a service industry, what is client feedback on the coachee like?

3

LISTEN TO FEEDBACK

Discuss the employee with colleagues and direct supervisors. You can gather opinions both from people who supervise the potential coachee and from the people who possibly work for the coachee. Make sure that you don't take all their opinions literally and try and understand the reasons some people have for appreciating or negatively criticizing the coachee. Some colleagues may be envious of the employee or merely be venting their own frustrations with their own work by focusing on another colleague.

4

RETURN TO OBSERVATION

Having done additional research, it could be useful to return to the observation stage just for one or two days to see if you look at the employee's working practices in a new light.

5

MAKE LIST

Once you have completed your research, you can make a list of positive and negative qualities of the coachee and identify some areas that will improve with coaching.

6

REVIEW TIMETABLE

Look at your diary and decide on a realistic time frame for the potential coaching session. See who is available to do the coaching. Will it be you directly, or will it be a trusted colleague who has already tackled a similar problem?

Establishing ground rules

You are now ready to take the next steps in the coaching cycle. The following to do list is based on the manager taking the initiative for the coaching, but a lot of it is still relevant and applicable if the employee has approached a manager with a request for coaching in one or more areas.

1 APPROACH THE EMPLOYEE
Contact the potential coachee and arrange a time for a meeting. You don't have to give a full explanation for the meeting, but it will help if the coachee is prepared to talk with you in some detail.

2

DECIDE ON MEETING PLACE

Book a room in the office to guarantee that you will be able to chat without interruptions for a period of time and in private. Alternatively, you could decide to meet in a café outside the office for a more neutral and informal setting. This may be preferable if the person you approach is particularly nervous or ill at ease.

3

MAKE OBSERVATIONS

Calmly and slowly relate the observations you have made in the last few weeks. Begin by stressing the positives of the employee's behavior and actions. Then turn to areas where you think they might benefit from coaching. Insist that your suggestions are aimed at improving performance and sustained career development rather than on rectifying possible defects.

Establishing ground rules continued

4

ASK FOR FEEDBACK

Ask the employee to give feedback on what they have just heard. If you are talking to a high achiever whom you want to promote, the response is likely to be positive, and you will be able to proceed to a plan of action fairly quickly. If you are discussing certain problems an employee is having with an area of her work, you must give the candidate extra time to digest your observations. The employee may become defensive, even hostile. Be ready for this response and allow them to ask any questions.

5

ARRANGE A FURTHER MEETING

If there are questions that need a more considered response, for you or the employee, and if the employee needs more time to consider what you have said, agree to postpone formulating an action plan until these issues are resolved. When the employee has taken on board your observations and is happy to proceed, move to an action plan.

6 AGREE ON ACTION

■ TO COACH OR NOT TO COACH?

The first point you need to agree on is that coaching will benefit the candidate. If the candidate is reluctant at this stage to accept the need for coaching, then you need to arrange another meeting.

■ WHAT TO COACH?

Although you are not ready to establish the details of the coaching program, you can broadly agree on one to three areas of their work that will benefit from coaching for instance: "finalizing a sale," "keeping records of account," or "acquiring management skills."

■ WHEN TO COACH?

You also need to establish the frequency of coaching sessions, the number of sessions, and the overall length of time required. Will it need a month? Three months? A two-day training session?

■ WHO WILL COACH?

Will you be directly responsible for coaching? Will the employee's supervisor? Are there advantages in hiring an external coach?

Goal-setting

Although you discussed goals when you laid down some ground rules, a second meeting is crucial to specify more clearly what the employee expects to gain from coaching. When a company imposes coaching on individuals through training sessions, the company goal has already been established. For instance, for a retailer, the objective could be "to raise sales by 10 percent during the Christmas selling period." The employees have no choice in the company's agenda. The most effective goal-setting, however, comes when a manager and a coachee agree together on set goals because the employee feels far more closely involved in the decision-making process. If the employee initiates the setting of the goal, then the incentive to achieve the ultimate objective will be even greater.

WHAT IF THE EMPLOYEE DOESN'T KNOW HIS OR HER OWN GOALS?

Although raising sales targets is a perfectly legitimate goal for a company, it may be too impersonal to motivate an individual. If a coach and employee can work together to incorporate a personal element into the company mission, then the situation can be beneficial for both parties.

For instance, an employee may decide that she wants to develop her own target for the Christmas sales period that exceeds the company's stated objective but not purely for the sake of an extra bonus but because she seeks a promotion to be head of the sales floor of her particular section. Immediately, you have two objectives: the literal one is to raise sales and the second one which touches career aspirations is to be given a promotion.

Not everyone however, has even these short-term goals either because they haven't been encouraged to think in terms of future objectives or because they are frightened of failure. Some questions you, as manager, can ask them in order to help them define some potential goals are listed on the following pages.

Goal-setting continued

SHORT-TERM PROFESSIONAL GOALS

1 Are you satisfied with your current salary, or do you think you deserve a raise?

2 Do you wish you were working for a different employer?

LONG-TERM PROFESSIONAL GOALS

1 Do you see yourself still with your present company in five years' time?

2 What sort of role would you like to be filling?

SHORT-TERM PERSONAL GOALS

1 Would you like to learn a new language?

2 Would you like to feel fitter? Should you join a gym?

LONG-TERM PERSONAL GOALS

1 Do you think you will remain in your current line of work?

2 Have you ever wanted to go back to school?

Goal-setting continued

Once you, as a manager, have a range of the coachee's professional and personal ambitions, you can write them down and identify if the objectives can be realistically attained through coaching. The objectives need to be SMART.

1

SPECIFIC
Can the employee define the goal in a brief phrase? For instance, it could be "to become head of sales in the department" or "to return to study."

2

MEASURABLE
Can you and the employee find out if the coachee has achieved her stated goal, for instance by being promoted within a year?

3

ATTAINABLE
How likely is it that the sales rep will become head of the department? Does she have a good track record? Are there other likely candidates?

4 REALISTIC
Has anyone else suggested she has the capability of leading a team?

5 TIME LIMITED
Does the employee have a certain time frame to achieve the goal? Is she prepared to wait six months at least but no longer than a year?

If the answer is “yes” to all five objectives, the goal that you and the employee eventually define can serve as an effective guide to action.

Identify tasks to achieve the goals

Now that coach and coachee have defined a goal they are ready to discuss a plan that is going to make the goals achievable. They need to answer the following questions:

1

What steps does the coachee have to take to reach her goal? Two immediate tasks can be identified:

- To examine current sales record and aim to reach a higher monthly target.
- To arrange a meeting with a line manager about ambitions. Bosses cannot guess what aspirations employees have. Sometimes, these have to be spelled out.

2

How long will it take to reach her objective?
In the case of raising sales, you can suggest three months to establish a sales pattern. The Christmas sales, which are important to the company, also create a deadline so that the employee can strive to do well during the sales period and approach a boss afterward.

3

What aspects of the job need to be improved?
This is where the benefits of coaching can most easily be felt. The employee may believe she has a good knowledge of the products she is selling but that her confidence in dealing with customers, particularly difficult ones, is rather low. She might benefit from coaching on customer service and how to be more assertive.

On the other hand, the employee may be good at dealing with clients but needs to learn more about the products she is selling. She might benefit from more knowledge on the actual products, so training in product descriptions, finishes, and so on will help her to serve her customers' needs more effectively, and ultimately raise sales.

Motivating employees

Motivating others means tapping into identifying the inner drive that compels them to succeed. Knowing what makes employees tick is a key skill for a coach because without the inner fire to want to achieve something, employees do not react, and coaches will achieve middling results at best. These are some recommended tips for effective motivating.

UNDERSTAND A WIDE RANGE OF DESIRES

What makes motivating others difficult is that everyone has different reasons to succeed, even when they are members of a tightly knit team. The first step in understanding others is to look at yourself and analyze what makes you tick at work. Be honest and write down at least one reason why you enjoy your present position. The following are common factors that motivate people in their professional life.

1

SOLVING PROBLEMS

Some people thrive on facing a tough situation and coming up with ways to solve it.

2

BEING CREATIVE

There are many ways of being creative that don't involve literally working in creative arts. Coming up with unusual ways of marketing a product or thinking of an innovative product line are ways of being creative. Even introducing a new filing system at work can get some people fired up.

Motivating employees continued

3

HELPING OTHERS

People in service industries enjoy working for others and providing a service from which they can see other people benefit.

4

TEACHING

Passing on information and seeing others develop is shared by teachers, coaches, and mentors.

5

RESEARCHING

For many people, the thrill of discovering new things keeps them at their job.

By understanding what makes people tick, you can better steer your strategy for motivating others. For instance, the person who likes being creative, is unlikely to benefit much from a course in administration. And the individual who loves research isn't a prime candidate for training in customer service. Try not to be guided by what you think people should like and learn from what is suitable for their type of personality and interests. Naturally, this can't be taken to extremes. If a new software system is being introduced and everyone in the department uses a computer, all employees will require coaching in the new system and regular technical updates.

Motivating employees continued

DON'T REWARD BAD BEHAVIOR

There are negative ways of motivating others. For instance, how many times have you seen an aggressive personality who always interrupts loudly, getting his own way because nobody dares to tell him to be quiet. Or how often does a new idea get knocked down by the office nit-picker who launches into a detailed criticism every time someone tries to introduce change? When managers fail to ignore these negative interruptions or try to put across an opposing view such as "well actually I think it's a very good idea," the people with bad behavior are encouraged to repeat their performances. At the same time, other colleagues who like coming up with ideas for instance, may be put off from repeating their positive efforts.

REWARD GOOD BEHAVIOR

Responding positively to good behavior is important for a manager because it shows employees that you are observing their actions and that you are appreciating their efforts. There are several ways of rewarding good behavior. They include:

- Offering positive feedback
- Giving some measure of public recognition
- Offering bonuses or incentives
- Leading by example
- Listening attentively
- Asking effective questions

We will look at each of these in turn in greater detail on the following pages.

Motivating employees continued

1

GIVE POSITIVE FEEDBACK

This is the most common way of acknowledging a good performance. Although sometimes, it can be done in public in a moment of spontaneity, it is better to arrange a private meeting. First, singling an employee out in public can cause problems to the person receiving the feedback who may prefer more intimacy and for others observing it who may resent not being the subject of the feedback even when they are also doing a good job. Second, a private meeting creates a more formal atmosphere where the person receiving the feedback can listen attentively to the feedback, ask questions, and, if the manager is taking notes, receive some official recognition of good work.

2

RECOGNIZE EMPLOYEE IN PUBLIC

Being recognized in public can be effective when it is done in a formal setting, for instance in an end-of-month meeting or annual company award ceremony where other attendees are specifically present to honor and acknowledge good work. Traditionally more common in sales industries than other settings, this approach to recognition can work in many sectors and is becoming more widespread.

Motivating employees continued

3

PROVIDE BONUS/INCENTIVES

Financial incentives work particularly well in sales-oriented businesses but less well in service industries where the way to quantify performance is slightly more objective and can lead to resentment among peers. The most successful approach in these areas is to offer a certain percentage of salary, or a fixed sum, to all staff. This, however, does not reward those team members who have delivered more.

4

LEAD BY EXAMPLE

Showing others how an assignment is handled can be a good way of motivating others, but a manager must not be seen to be performing well for an audience. The way of working efficiently should come across as genuine. Employees are far more prone to pick up on managers who are not leading by example rather than those who are doing a good job. So managers must be careful to practice what they preach. If a manager is cutting corners or missing deadlines, you can be sure that employees will be encouraged to follow suit.

5

BE A GOOD LISTENER

Listening effectively does not only involve giving employees some set time to listen to their problems. The manager has to follow up these listening sessions with some concrete evidence that he has taken on board some of the messages that employees were giving him. For instance, if an employee is complaining to a manager about the lack of opportunities for business travel, and the manager does nothing to alter the situation or to explain why business trips won't be available for a certain period, then the employee will feel she wasn't being listened to, however long the meeting was.

6

ASK QUESTIONS

Company questionnaires asking employees what they think about certain aspects of their work won't really be enough. A manager must ask personal questions in a setting where the employee has time to think of what he is being asked. This means setting up periodic meetings with employees. Write down any answers because it not only shows you are being attentive, but it will help you to remember what the employee's main concerns were.

Delegating

Delegating means handing over authority to a member of your team to carry out part of your job. As the manager, you are still ultimately responsible if the job goes wrong, which is one of the main reasons why delegating proves difficult for some managers. However, there are some clear benefits for both manager and subordinates in delegating work.

1

TO MOTIVATE STAFF

Handing over new tasks to subordinates shows that you trust their ability to take on new projects. You may be surprised by how positively staff respond by doing a good job.

2

TO STRENGHTEN TEAM SPIRIT

When other people in your team get involved with some of your tasks, they can understand some of your objectives more clearly. People pull together more when they feel they are striving for the same goal.

3

TO FREE YOUR TIME FOR OTHER ROLES

As manager, your responsibilities are numerous, and by farming out some of your tasks, you have the chance to focus on another pressing job that needs special attention.

4

TO REDUCE STAFF TURNOVER

Work out how many people may have left the company or the department in the last year. Have people been leaving because they are seeking responsibilities that they are not getting from you? Delegating can reduce staff turnover.

5

TO FOCUS ON CORE JOB

Your job has many responsibilities, but at certain moments, there is a pressing job that needs special attention. By farming out some of your responsibilities, you have the opportunity to focus on what matters most for the business.

How to hand over tasks

1

IDENTIFYING WHAT TASKS TO DELEGATE

The first step is to identify what aspects of your work you can hand over by writing a list of all your tasks and crossing off the ones that you are totally responsible for and would require too much coaching at this stage.

For the smaller tasks:

- Analyze how much training is involved in handing over the task. Also identify how much time a coaching session would take. You don't want to put people off by overwhelming them with a responsibility that has to be carried out in a short space of time.

- Look also at whether there are regular tasks that must be carried out that would require only minimal coaching time. For example, does a monthly report have to be created in a standard format. Once you have explained the template and where an employee can find the figures he needs, it is a straightforward task to hand over the writing of the report for the foreseeable future.

2

IDENTIFY WHOM TO DELEGATE TASKS TO
This process demands writing several lists.

- The first is one of people who have actively been asking for extra responsibilities in recent months.

- The second is one of people who are literally available in the next few months and not overcommitted in other tasks. Maybe an expected assignment has been shelved or otherwise delayed and you have employees who are currently undercommitted.

- The third is a list of people who have the skills and the track record to handle extra tasks or who have potential that you could develop.

From these three lists, there should emerge a short list of names that appear more than once. That is your starting point in selecting candidates ready for delegation.

Handing over the task

There are three main stages in the process of delegating: hand over, monitoring, and providing feedback.

Once you've pinpointed the task you want to hand over and who you want to carry it out, approach the candidate with a brief and ask whether he or she is interested in the job.

1 Define the limits of authority that you are handing over. The candidate will need freedom to carry out the task, but you need to explain that the final responsibility is yours.

2 Define a time frame for the task.

3 Ask the candidate if he or she requires any special training.

4 Advise other staff that the candidate will be carrying out the task so that everyone involved is aware.

5 Advise the candidate of sources of information that might be useful, as well as people who may prove helpful in undertaking the task. Invite contributions from the candidate on potential sources of information he or she can identify.

Monitoring the task

It is always in the manager's best interest for the chosen candidate to accomplish the task effectively since:

- A wise appointment reflects well on the manager.
- A task well done means the staff member can be relied on for future assignments.
- Staff will be motivated by the successful example of a fellow member doing a good job.

To ensure you are providing sufficient support to the staff member:

1

DEFINE BRIEF
However obvious the role of the assignment may be, it is worth defining in a sentence or two what you expect the candidate to accomplish and to establish some markers that measure progress.

2

ESTABLISH MEETING TIMES

Agree on a fixed time during the day or week (depending on the length of the assignment) to meet up with the candidate so that you both have the opportunity to ask questions and to catch up and report on progress.

3

CHECK TRAINING

If the candidate asked for special coaching, make sure this happens some time in advance of taking on the task. Depending on the availability of coaches, training can take time to set up. Even if the candidate hasn't asked for training, make sure you explain any methods or procedures that must be followed in completing the assignment.

Provide feedback

The manager needs to tell the worker how he has performed to instill confidence and trust, which the manager can make use of in the future.

1

WRITE A REPORT

It is very useful to provide a written report describing what the worker accomplished and how this compared to the targets set by the manager.

2

ANALYZE SHORTCOMINGS

If there were shortcomings, point them out but try to explain why they occurred. Overall, try to be as positive and encouraging as possible.

3

INVITE QUESTIONS

You should encourage the candidate to provide his own feedback of the job, how well he felt he was supervised, and whether he would like to take on any similar assignments in the future.

4

IDENTIFY TRAINING NEEDS

The project may well have shown that further training would be desirable. If this is the case, discuss what should be done, and schedule it in. If you want the employee to undertake similiar tasks, without shortcomings, you must ensure that any training is carried out.

Employees without ambition

There are special considerations to keep in mind when coaching good employees with no ambitions.

WHO ARE THEY

There are some types of employees who simply aren't interested in furthering themselves but nevertheless do their jobs satisfactorily enough. You, as a manager, could decide that it is best to leave these types of workers and focus instead on:

- The high achievers who actively seek to advance themselves in the company
- The problem cases who need to be coached if they don't want to lose their jobs

WHY THEY ARE USEFUL

For a start, steady employees who plod along in their jobs for years are useful in many ways:

- They seem satisfied where they are, and this satisfaction spreads to co-workers.
- They know the inner workings of the company.
- They may have chosen to do a job that doesn't stretch them because they have other ambitions outside work and do not want extra responsibilities at work to distract from these.
- They may simply be at home with the security of the situation they know.

As a manager, don't underestimate how useful it is to have reliable workers who fulfill necessary functions and who are not going to rock the boat.

Employees without ambition continued

However, you still have a lot to gain from trying to push these good employees with no ambition. These are some recommended steps to follow.

1

COURT THEM

These types of employees have reached their positions by not making a lot of fuss and just getting on with it, so they won't be used to having a manager give them special attention. It's worthwhile not to ignore them because you don't want these reliable types to leave the company.

2

IDENTIFY POSITIVES

Apart from being valuable assets because they do their jobs satisfactorily and they don't make demands, try to think of other positive qualities they have such as being efficient at accounts or good at following up complaints from customers, or good team players.

3

EXPAND HORIZONS

Having identified the positives, you can meet up with these employees, underline their strengths, and ask them whether they would like to take on extra responsibilities that are directly related to their strengths. If they tolerate what they usually do, the chances are that they will be happy taking on extra work that plays to these same strengths.

4

EXPLORE TRAINING POTENTIAL

If they are not so eager to pile on more tasks, you might ask them if they are willing to show others how they do their job. Explain that they could serve as role models for other workers doing the same job in different departments. You might tap into a desire to teach or to share their existing skills.

Giving negative feedback

Providing feedback is an essential part of management because it is the most direct way an employee can find out how she is performing. It typically takes the form of a face-to-face conversation and occurs every six months, sometimes once a year, or at key stages of a project.

Feedback is much easier when a manager has positive things to say about a candidate, but it is considerably more difficult when an employee is not performing to the best of her ability. The three most common consequences in this situation tend to be:

1 The manager puts off the feedback session but is only delaying the inevitable.

2 The manager has the session and mentions the criticisms briefly but, to avoid confrontation, keeps the meeting short, causing only confusion in the employee who may seek more detailed explanation for the analysis or needs time to voice her own opinions.

3 The manager is so frustrated with the employee's performance that he focuses too heavily on shortcomings without offering advice or suggestions about how to improve or eliciting information from the employee on what training needs could be addressed.

Giving negative feedback continued

The following steps are recommended to ensure that a feedback session is beneficial to both manager and employee, mainly by encouraging an improved performance in the future. The assumption is that the individual receiving the feedback has underperformed. However, the same steps can be followed for a worker who has performed well.

1

DO THOROUGH HOMEWORK

There is nothing more demotivating for the employee receiving criticism than an underprepared manager who makes broad criticisms based on allegations or rumors and without backing his criticisms with specific examples. Find out from other colleagues why the employee's work is considered unsatisfactory. Be discreet: you do not want the rumor mill to go into overdrive.

2

KNOW EMPLOYEE'S PERSONALITY

A manager doesn't have to know intimate details about the employee in question, but it is useful for the manager to have a general knowledge of the individual so that he can modify his delivery according to the basic personality type of the employee. Ask yourself such questions as:

- Is the employee an introvert and likely to be silent during the meeting?
- Is the individual volatile and you expect him to lash back in anger? Be ready then for a long, defensive speech.

3

REHEARSE DELIVERY

It is wise to write down the main points that you are going to cover and to look through the notes before the meeting. You could even quickly rehearse your delivery, even if only in your head. You as manager are the person who is setting the agenda and tone of the meeting, but you should not sound staged. Your job is also to listen to the employee's explanations for the underperformance.

Giving negative feedback continued

4

CHOOSE PRIVATE LOCATION

Never provide feedback in a public place and certainly not in an office room in front of colleagues. Make sure the employee is warned about the meeting a few days in advance so he too has time to prepare. Book a quiet room, and make sure that you are not available during the session.

5

GET TO THE POINT

Once at the meeting, don't spend too much time on preambles. Be direct. Try "I have asked you here because I want to discuss your performance...." You need to focus on one issue at a time. If you address too many concerns, the employee may feel overwhelmed.

6 AVOID CRITICIZING THE PERSON

When you go on to spell out the performance, dwell on the employee's actions or behavior that needs improving. Steer away from any personal comments or pointing a finger at the person. For instance, "The report you wrote could be improved by adding more details on x and would be clearer if a summary were added" is much easier to hear, more specific, and more useful than "You aren't very good at writing reports. We expected more from you."

7 BE READY FOR ANGER

A defensive response is natural in many people, and you can expect some criticism directed at you. Don't respond in the same manner, even if you are challenged directly. This is an opportunity for the person to get things off his chest. Listen carefully and take notes.

Giving negative feedback continued

8

BE READY FOR SILENCE

Passive employees may curl up inside and sulk. In the same way that you allow an angry person to vent his frustration for a minute or so, you could chose to wait a little for the individual to open up. Don't ask them immediately to give an opinion. Try to think of a few open-ended questions to get them to start responding. "Do you think what I have described is unfair?" only invites a "yes" or "no" answer. It is better to say: "I understand that you may think what I have said is unfair. If you think so, I would like to hear your side of the story."

9

SUGGEST ACTION PLAN

The best action plans are conjured up together. You can try to ask the employee what steps he thinks he could take to improve performance. Only if there is no response, can you suggest a few options. Even in this case, let him decide which he could try first. You need the employee's collaboration to achieve success.

10

DOCUMENT CONVERSATION

You should never leave the meeting without a record of the conversation. The first reason is that, in the case of an extremely angry and defensive employee, he may retaliate with a different account of the meeting, potentially using the distorted account as a basis for disciplinary action. In addition, a recorded document makes it much easier for reference purposes for a second meeting.

11

FOLLOW UP

After the meeting, it is a good idea to type out any notes and send the employee a written summary of what was discussed with any suggestions for improving behavior or performance. This is the time to arrange a follow-up meeting.

Following up

Following up marks the final stage of the coaching process. Following up does not have to be restricted to one session and is often more effective if it is on-going. In most cases, there is no one particular ending point to coaching, but a series of final sessions that deal with separate issues.

WHY IS FOLLOW UP IMPORTANT?

1 Any coaching program needs to have specific time boundaries and a follow-up session that has been arranged well in advance, but it also must provide a focus for both the coach and the coachee to achieve what they set out to do.

2 A final session gives both parties the opportunity to measure exactly how much has been achieved, how it was achieved, what is still missing, and what can be done to fill the gaps.

3 A follow-up meeting also presents both parties with an effective motivational tool. In an ideal scenario, most of what coaching aims to accomplish has been achieved, and coach and coachee can commend each other on having reached their goals. This moves the relationship forward.

Following up continued

The final procedure is typically as follows:

1

ARRANGE FOLLOW-UP MEETING
This should be arranged well in advance. Set a realistic date. There is no point in attending a follow-up meeting if the coachee still feels there is a long way to go unless she is seriously stuck and needs the meeting to fix things.

2

WRITE REVIEW
For the coach, it is useful to refer to the original notes of the first meeting, examine the intermediate and final goals and tasks that were laid out, and make ticks and any additional comments beside each of them.

3

BE REALISTIC
If there were several short-term goals required to achieve one long-term goal, be realistic in writing your review. Some minigoals will have been achieved; others may not. This does not invalidate the process or the way forward.

4

INVITE DISCUSSION

Whatever conclusions you may have come to, allow the employee first to give her own opinion on how successful or otherwise the coaching has been. Ask open-ended questions like “So how do you think it has worked?” rather than a leading question like “Well you must be pleased?” or “This is rather disappointing, don’t you think?”

5

AGREE ON CONCLUSION

Unless you agree to disagree—and this would happen only when the coaching process has failed—you can try to summarize the main results and benefits of the coaching session.

6

RESET GOALS

Improving performance is never ending, and after agreeing on a conclusion, the employee may decide to set a new target that may involve further coaching with you, the previous coach, or a new coach.

A look at a coaching session

OVERVIEW

There is no single template for a coaching session. The shape and length of a coaching session will vary widely depending on the number of people being coached, the nature of the problem, and the time available for the coaching session.

CASE STUDY

Assume for the purpose of illustration, the case of the new manager, Brad Turner (see pp. 54–55, 84–85, and 106–107), who has recently been promoted from sales executive to director of sales at a multinational hotel resort in a major business destination.

Brad's line manager, also the general manager of the hotel, has requested that Brad attend a coaching session on the food and beverage part of Brad's overall assignment. He has given Brad three days' notice for the session to prepare any questions. The session has been timed during the least busy part of the day (8–9 a.m.) to avoid as many interruptions as possible.

THE COACHING SESSION FOLLOWS FOUR MAIN STEPS:

1. ESTABLISHING A GOAL

The coach's first mission is to instill a sense of purpose for the meeting by underlining the main challenge facing Brad.

GENERAL MANAGER: So Brad, we are here to discuss your main responsibilities concerning sales of food and beverage. I know we have other areas to cover, but we will handle those sessions later this week. My concern now is that the department has been underperforming. [This is a description of the problem in brief.] Let's go through the department's five main areas of revenue: room service, the Royal Café, the Coconut Grove, the Japanese Experience, and the Criterion. [This specifies the main problem areas.] Have you been able to consult the different venue heads? [This invites a response from Brad.]

BRAD: Yes, I have talked to the various heads and gone through some of the revenue figures of the last four months. Overall, room service continues to perform well and the Royal Café attracts a number of breakfast customers, both from the hotel and from surrounding offices. But the Coconut Grove (Caribbean drinks and dishes) and the Japanese Experience (sushi bar) are only half full on weekdays. And the Criterion is receiving fewer corporate bookings.

A look at a coaching session continued

It looks to me, that we need to work toward turning around these last three venues and raise afternoon visits at the Royal Café. [This specifies further the problem, outlining priorities.] We all seem to agree that a time frame of three months is appropriate to evaluate whether we need to change the products and whether our sales teams are tapping the appropriate target customers. Does that sound correct? [Seeking confirmation.]

2. RAISING POSSIBLE HYPOTHESIS
GENERAL MANAGER: At this stage, what do you think are the main problems with the various venues? Don't worry, I won't hold you to the answer. I'm interested in your opinion. [It is important to start thinking about options.]

BRAD: This is only a hunch but as far as the Japanese restaurant is concerned, a few Asian-style fusion eateries have opened in the area in recent months.

GENERAL MANAGER: Have you visited these other places?

BRAD: No.

3. INVITING OPTIONS/STRATEGIES
GENERAL MANAGER: It would be a good idea to visit them all and make a price comparison. Also check the type of clientele. In fact, it could be a good idea for you and some of your sales executives to do the same with the other venues. For instance, how many cafés are we competing with in the area? Could that be affecting

afternoon visits at the Café Royal? [A call for action: making a price comparison.]

[A new suggestion follows.]
GENERAL MANAGER: Have you met up with the finance department yet? They should go through all the financial statements of each individual restaurant, and we can find out whether we are paying too much for certain food products. Would you like me to arrange a meeting? [A call for further coaching: on financial statements.]

Would it also be useful to arrange a meeting with each of the restaurant chefs? You can find out what their feedback is on the general situation.

BRAD: Yes. [Call for further action and information gathering.]

4. WRAPPING UP
[This is the time for the general manager to sum up.]

GENERAL MANAGER: So, we've agreed on a timetable. I've jotted down the main venues that concern us, and I think you know what questions you want to be answered. I will confirm the meetings with the finance director and the food chefs by this afternoon. Is there anything else that concerns you? If not, let's agree to meet next week to find out how you are progressing. [This summarizes the main points while still inviting further questions and initiatives from Brad.]

Improving your coaching skills

In the same way that most people in the workplace never stop benefiting from effective coaching, so the people providing the coaching never stop developing their own skills as teachers, trainers, mentors, and communicators.

These are some recommended steps to follow to keep updating your coaching skills.

1

ATTEND SEMINARS/CONFERENCES

Coaches may be experts in their chosen subject, but there are always developments in their fields and it is worth making a list of key conferences and seminars to attend in your city/area during the year. Listening to other people in the field is a way to check that you are up to speed with any new ways of thinking as well as a way to challenge your current thoughts and opinions.

2

ASK FOR FEEDBACK

It may be intimidating to ask coachees for feedback on your sessions, but how else are you going to know what your strong and weak areas are? Encourage people you have coached to make any positive and negative comments about your coaching so that you can identify what you might need to improve on and what you should continue to practice. Don't forget that what works for one candidate, won't necessarily succeed with another.

3

OBSERVE BEHAVIOR

Not all coaches have the privilege of being able to witness improvements in their coachees unless they work in the same organization. Even if you don't work in the same company, try to follow up on any former coachees a few months after a coaching session has ended to record what progress has been made.

Improving your coaching skills continued

4 RESEARCH

You can never read too much about your specialized subject or areas of interest. Try to subscribe to the leading magazines or journals that cover your area or arrange to, at the very least, have monthly access to them by visiting specialized institutes or trade associations.

5 SELF-COACH

Practice what you preach to your coachees. Take the GROW (Goal, Reality, Options, Wrap-up) model used by many coaches. When was the last time you sat down and asked yourself about your own goals and objectives and how you are going about fulfilling them? Have your goals changed slowly without you consciously knowing about it?

6

BE POSITIVE

One of the ultimate aims of coaching others, whatever the field, is to instill a positive attitude in others. The best way of spreading a positive message is to be positive oneself. Do you think of a challenge as a problem or an opportunity? Do you remind yourself that for most challenges, there are several options available?

7

BE CREATIVE

It is a fallacy that you are either creative or not. You can force yourself to think outside the box by challenging the assumptions of your coachee, of the business environment he works in, and even of yourself. You can also practice various techniques to overcome barriers to creative thinking such as brainstorming, Mind Mapping®, and six thinking hats.

Buying in coaching

WHY BUY-IN A COACH?

1. You are already a coach but have identified a skills gap.
2. You have defined an area for which you need training.

HOW DO I LOOK FOR A COACH?

1. PERSONAL RECOMMENDATIONS
Ask friends and colleagues.

PRO: You know that the coach has achieved results, and your access may be quicker from a word of mouth recommendation.
CON: What works for your friend may not work with you. Your research may be less thorough.

2. CONFERENCE, SEMINARS
Attend meetings and seminars.

PRO: You are able to identify relevant players in your sector or industry and witness their style, thoughts, and delivery first hand.
CON: Some people are effective public speakers but less able to handle a one-to-one relationship.

3. INTERNET SEARCH
Try conducting a search on your favorite search engines.

PRO: You can shop around, regardless of location. You are also able to compare prices.
CON: You may be influenced by the quality of the web site. You have no direct recommendation.

WHAT SHOULD I LOOK FOR IN A COACH?

1

SPECIALIST OR GENERALIST?

Are you looking for specific advice, for instance a particular aspect of finance or computing where you need a specialist, or for more general advice such as decision making or delegating work where you may be better off with a generalist?

2

EXPERIENCE

How long has the coach been training others? Asking this question doesn't mean you automatically prefer coaches with more than, say, three years experience. You may also want to look at what sort of job the potential coach was doing before he become a part-time or full-time coach. Sometimes, his experience may prove the deciding factor.

DON'T BE AFRAID TO:

TEST-RUN

Suggest a trial period with the coach. After all, the coach may also be testing you out to see if the match-up works for both sides.

SHORTLIST

Target a list of no fewer than three potential candidates so you feel confident you are making an informed choice.

6

mentoring in action

The stages of mentoring

This chapter looks at the different stages of the mentoring relationship from both the mentee's and the mentor's points of view. The stages are broadly as follows:

1. The conception: how the mentor and mentee find each other and agree to embark on a relationship.

2. The development of the relationship, which involves establishing goals, challenging assumptions, and building confidence in the mentee and the relationship.

3. The closure of the relationship and how to make sure the end of the relationship is positive, not negative.

YOU AS MENTEE: FINDING A MENTOR

With companies that provide formal mentoring, choosing a mentor is the responsibility of your boss or senior management. In some companies, there will be a pool of senior exectives who take on this role.

The following section is aimed at people who don't enjoy this formal framework or even for those in a formal mentoring program who are seeking to complement their existing arrangement by drawing on wider experience.

Finding a mentor: practicalities

These are recommended steps to follow:

1 NARROW FOCUS

Before your search begins, you need to identify exactly what area of your job or career you want guidance in. If you are a banker, are you interested, for instance, in investment, consumer, or international banking?

2 READ AROUND THE SUBJECT

Once you've specified your areas of interest, read as much as possible about the subject in periodicals, trade magazines, and books. Note down the names and departments of any senior directors in the field. The leaders who are geographically closer to your city will be the main targets although there are examples of distance mentoring.

3 ASK QUESTIONS

Colleagues, bosses, and other people in competing companies can provide a wealth of information about some of the leading and up-and-coming authorities in your area of greatest interest.

4

ATTEND SEMINARS

Attending conferences and seminars can also provide an immediate way of not just reading and knowing about potential mentors, but actually talking to them.

5

JOIN TRADE ASSOCIATIONS

Joining trade associations can be useful to meet senior figures in your sector, particularly those who have retired from top positions and have more time to devote to promoting the industry and teaching others.

6

USE OFFICIAL MENTOR RESOURCES

The Service Corps of Retired Executives (SCORE) provides names and programs related to mentoring. SCORE also offers free e-mail counseling. The Office of Women's Business Ownership matches mentees with experienced women mentors.

Finding a mentor

WHAT YOU IDEALLY SEEK IN A MENTOR

While you are taking practical steps to research the best mentor for you (including points such as is the mentor available? does he have time?), it is useful to have the following list of ideal characteristics of a mentor to compare with any potential candidates. Not all mentors can possess all these qualities, but they should have a degree of skill in the majority. This list will also serve as a checklist for would-be mentors:

1 HIGH ACHIEVER

If you have drawn a list of potential candidates from some of the most successful or admired leaders in your industry, they are inevitably going to be high achievers. People who strive for the best in their profession tend to thrive on taking extra responsibilities and have unusual drive to succeed.

2

PASSIONATE TEACHER

Not all high achievers are effective at helping others accomplish the same thing, particularly the ones who are too driven with their own personal ambition. Neither are they necessarily patient with those who still have a lot to learn about a trade or business. That's why to find a high achiever who has the time, patience, and willingness to share their learning is fairly unusual.

3

PEOPLE PERSON

Some high achievers are excellent at producing results but still not good at managing people. An effective mentor must have people skills such as being a sympathetic listener and perceptive about others' motivations as well as their other strengths and weaknesses.

Finding a mentor continued

4

EXCELLENT MOTIVATOR

Many high achievers know exactly what makes them tick and what drives them to strive for the best, but they can't necessarily goad others to do the same. Motivating others is an acquired skill and is closely related to being interested in other people.

5

CONFIDENT BUSINESSPERSON

A mentor needs to be confident in her own abilities and achievements to give her time and energy to helping another individual without feeling threatened by the mentee. She must also actively enjoy seeing others improve.

6

EXCELLENT NETWORKER

One of a mentor's most helpful contributions to an individual who is starting out in his profession is to introduce the mentee to other valuable contacts in the sector who can provide further assistance and possibly job openings.

7

GENEROUS ADVISOR

Because the majority of mentors will be directors or managers toward the end of their careers when they could be spending much more time on leisurely pursuits, it takes a considerable amount of generosity to want to help another person for no financial gain.

Finding a mentee

YOU AS A MENTOR: FINDING A MENTEE

The majority of mentor relationships, unless they are imposed by a company that deliberately nurtures the practice of mentoring, will spring from the mentee who seeks outs the mentor. This doesn't ignore those occasions when senior managers decide to take a new employee with potential under their wings. The personal and professional benefits for doing so are numerous, as identified in Chapter 4. In such cases, part of the decision to recruit is that the individual will need mentoring, and this has been factored into the decision to make a job offer.

IDENTIFYING A MENTEE

However, the mentoring relationships is a two-way dialog between two people. Even if the mentee is, in most cases, the initiator, the mentor also should know what the ideal characteristics of a mentee are. Although not all mentees will possess all these characteristics, having at least half of them will significantly improve the chances of a successful relationship. Mentoring relies on mutual respect. Although being similar types of people is not essential, valuing the characteristics that each brings to the relationship is. Some of the most common character traits a mentor may look for in a mentee are outlined in the following pages.

Finding a mentee continued

1

AMBITIOUS BUSINESSPERSON

High-achieving managers are likely to identify ambition in fairly junior staff as they themselves must have shown the same drive to succeed when they started their careers.

2

EAGER STUDENT

Just as the mentor should show all the best qualities of a good teacher, so the mentee must be a student who is keen to develop new skills. This may mean that the mentee will have less spare time or will run the danger of doing less well initially as he or she tackles new tasks.

3

TEAM PLAYER

Most top leaders have been able to work in a team while climbing up the corporate ladder and a mentee will ideally show the same ability to negotiate with you as a mentor and with his peers in general. Team playing qualities include:

- Being able to accept praise and criticism
- Being able to resolve differences between conflicting members of the team
- Identifying strengths and weaknesses in others and pointing them out to the team
- Listening to others' opinions
- Not being unduly influenced by others for the sake of personal popularity

Finding a mentee continued

4

RISK TAKER
Mentees already show unusual resolve and initiative with their decision to seek out a mentor. This lack of fear in challenging situations should be encouraged by mentors. Few top managers have reached their positions without taking some chances.

5

PATIENT WORKER
A mentee must have realistic expectations of what he will gain from a mentoring relationship. An individual who wants results too quickly or who is not prepared to endure an element of grind to achieve success will be a difficult mentee to work with.

6

REALIST

Mentees who show healthy optimism based on realistic expectations and an ability to get up after any serious setback will be far easier to guide than candidates who have a fear of failure.

7

VISIONARY

A mentee needs to have a vision of himself as a success in the future. Most top leaders have had vision—of themselves, of a product, of a successful business.

Matching mentor to mentee

THE MENTEE:
These are some practical steps for a typical mentee to follow to contact potential mentors.

1

REVIEW RESEARCH
If you followed most of the steps on pp. 177–179, you should now have a list of prospective mentors with their telephone numbers and e-mail/postal addresses.

2

REDEFINE GOALS
You should also have a written statement of no more than two or three sentences outlining what your objectives are. For instance: "I am seeking guidance on how to use my sales skills to move into a senior management role that will also involve financial and administrative experience, which I don't have."

3 MATCH GOALS WITH MENTOR LIST

Rank the list of potential mentors in order of relevance to your statement of intent.

4 WRITE E-MAILS/LETTERS

Write a letter to the top five candidates explaining that you are interested in a relationship with them by outlining in a sentence or two why you have chosen them and including your written "goal" statement.

Matching mentor to mentee continued

5

FOLLOW UP WITH CALL

After a reasonable period of time, you can call the candidates to ask if they have received the letter/e-mail and wait for their response.

6

ARRANGE MEETING

Assuming positive feedback from at least one candidate, arrange a meeting. You can suggest meeting outside the office in a neutral environment. You should insist on paying for any coffee/drinks.

7

APPROACH MEETING AS JOB INTERVIEW

You should take any meeting with a mentor seriously and do as much preparation as possible to give a good impression. At the same time, you are interviewing them so don't be afraid to take copious notes. Ask about:

- Their availability
- Level of interest
- Career history

Don't be afraid to explain that you are interested in their input and finding out whether they want to plan a second meeting with a view to establishing a longer term relationship with you.

Matching mentor to mentee continued

8

BE PATIENT WITH RESPONSE
High-flying managers are inevitably going to be very busy so don't despair if a reply isn't instantaneous. In the meantime, send a note thanking the candidate for his time, with a brief reminder of your objectives.

9

KEEP OPTIONS OPEN
At this preliminary stage, while you are waiting for feedback, there is nothing wrong with arranging a meeting with another potential mentor.

10

GET WRITTEN AGREEMENT

The need for a written agreement may seem somewhat binding considering that the relationship is only just beginning, but a straightforward statement of intent doesn't have to appear threatening to either party. Include such factors as:

- Your goals
- Nature of contact, for example, will you meet face to face, or will the mentor be available to answer e-mail or telephone queries
- Date to review relationship

In a formal mentoring arrangement, follow this up with a contract (see p. 196).

Formal mentoring

When a formal mentoring relationship is established by the company, the following elements are often present:

1

FORMAL CONTRACT
An official understanding between mentor and protégé will outline the main expectations and obligations of the two participants.

2

TRAINING
The company arranging the mentor relationship (typically internally) will provide training so that both mentor and mentee understand their roles.

3

MONITORING

The company will have a monitoring system in place, usually undertaken by a third party to make sure both sides are happy with the arrangement and that guidelines are being followed.

4

EVALUATION

The company will also provide an evaluation at the end of the mentoring program to summarize the main achievements and potential setbacks.

Mentoring session for a new manager

WHAT A MENTORING SESSION LOOKS LIKE

OVERVIEW: There are no typical mentoring sessions, particularly as the length and form of mentoring sessions depends entirely on the length of the relationship between mentor and mentee and on the immediate needs of the mentee.

CASE STUDY: In this example, the new manager, Brad Turner, has recently been promoted to head of sales at a major hotel chain. Although he is undergoing a series of practical and technical coaching sessions with various heads of departments, he has one long-term concern about his career that he is unable to tackle during these sessions. As a result, he has asked to meet with a former general manager of a rival hotel who now works as a part-time consultant, for an initial mentoring session. They have decided to meet at a neutral place: the lobby of a hotel with no connections to Brad or his mentor.

THE SESSION

IDENTIFYING MAIN CONCERNS

MENTOR: So how are you getting on in your new role? [This invites Brad to talk about his current position, the immediate challenges, and potential frustrations, and for the mentor to begin to gauge Brad's overall attitude to his job.]

MENTOR: Are you satisfied with the coaching sessions you are getting? [If Brad shows he is fairly happy with the coaching for his new role, the mentor can ask another general question like:] Do you see yourself being sales head for some time? Have you thought of your next step?

BRAD: I've only ever worked in this hotel chain and although I like the company and feel I have made a lot of progress within it, I think that I might benefit from a hotel with a different approach. [This specifies his main reason for calling the meeting.]

MENTOR AS SPONSOR

MENTOR: I could put you in touch with a couple of senior managers who have worked in different environments. They could tell you more about the challenges of moving across hotel cultures. [The mentor as a sponsor, pp. 214–215.]

MENTOR AS CAREER ADVISOR

MENTOR: Can I make another recommendation? [Now, the mentor steps in the role of a career advisor.] Why don't you take a few days leave from your work when it is reasonable and spend a day talking to these managers in the actual hotels. That will give you a better feel about a new hotel culture. You can learn a lot in a day or two and you might have a clearer picture of what style you prefer. [The mentor is giving career advice here, see pp. 220–223.]

Do you want to think about that option and we can meet again when you've decided? [Brad agrees.] We can pencil in another date now and discuss your progress then? [Giving the mentee the initiative.]

Informal mentoring

In more informal mentoring, which is the main subject of this chapter, such a formal guideline doesn't exist. Many elements of the formal mentoring process can be followed. It depends on mentor and protégé how far they want to take the process.

It is important to have a framework in which to work. There is unlikely to be a third party in this sort of relationship: mentor and mentee have to agree on the way forward. These are some suggestions for reaching an agreement.

1

ESTABLISH ROUTINE

Without a formal arrangement, it is dangerously easy for both sides to shift meeting times depending on delayed deadlines or unexpected demands. Obviously, both sides have to be flexible, but it is imperative to try to stick to some time structure as much as possible. It is best to:

- Set a time of the week or month that is mutually convenient and stick to it rigidly unless there is a real emergency.
- Arrange to meet at a given place, either in the office or outside, and make sure the venue is booked in good time, if this is necessary.

2

DISCUSS EXPECTATIONS

Make sure that both parties understand why they are getting together. The protégé is best advised to put his or her expectations in writing. If the mentee doesn't offer a statement, the mentor can also draw these out by asking:

- What does the mentee expect to gain from this relationship in the short and longer term?
- Does the mentor want to gain anything from the relationship, or is it purely altruistic?
- How can we work together? Will we have weekly, bi-monthly, monthly meetings?
- What are your career ambitions?

3

UNDERSTAND MENTOR/MENTEE ROLES

An appreciation of some of the main roles that each side takes is also vital for a smooth relationship, see the following pages.

Mentee's mission

The mentee may not always be aware of the roles he or she is expected to perform under the assumption that the mentor has the real initiative in the relationship. These are some guidelines for mentees to follow.

1 HAVE A GOAL

As discussed earlier, the importance of establishing a goal cannot be underestimated as a way to provide direction and personal motivation. Because your mentor is not necessarily in your company and is looking at your overall development, you should try to be open about all your personal and professional goals, both short term and long term. Questions to ask yourself can include: "Do you see yourself in your present company in five years time?"/ "What sort of role would you like to be doing?"/ "Have you contemplated working on your own or on a freelance basis?"/ "Do you wish you were working for a different employer?"/ "Have you ever thought you wanted a completely different career but feel compelled to stay in your current sector because of pressures from family and friends?"/ "Should you take up some hobbies to achieve a better work/life balance?"

2

PREPARE, PREPARE

There is nothing more off-putting for the mentor who has taken precious time to meet a mentee than for the mentee to show up to a meeting unprepared and without an agenda. You, as a mentee, have embarked on this relationship, and the least you can do is take it seriously. Show up to the meeting with pen, paper, possibly a tape recorder. Make sure you review your notes after the meeting and that you refer to the previous meeting and its conclusions.

Mentee's mission continued

3

RECIPROCATE INTEREST

The main focus of the mentor/mentee relationship will be the protégé but that is no reason that the mentee can't make an effort to show considerable interest in the mentor. Find out what projects the mentor is working on and ask a few questions about how it's progressing. The mentor won't expect to launch into great detail about his other activities, but he will appreciate your interest. The relationship can only benefit from mutual concern and consideration. This sensitivity may be essential later when you both have important deadlines that may make sticking to your agreed schedule more tricky.

4

COMMUNICATE EFFECTIVELY

Being a good communicator involves effective listening, which shows you are taking on board the other person's opinions and informing the mentor of any developments you have made. Don't let him know of a vital job interview two weeks after the event, for instance.

5 SHOW AWARENESS OF MENTOR'S TIME

Particularly in the beginning of the relationship, when both sides are testing the waters, you should make sure that the length of meetings and their frequency are suitable to the mentor. Don't presume that the mentor has unlimited time to chat with you. An hour might be all he can spare in a week and if that is the case, respect this limit by not extending it or arriving late. Arrange the venue for his convenience to cut down on travel time. Once you both know each other, you will know whether the mentor is open to longer meetings, perhaps over lunch or dinner.

6 LEARN TO INTERPRET

At the beginning of the relationship, your rambling thoughts and questions may require some steering by the mentor, but once you have started to gain knowledge and experience, you should learn to analyze issues yourself.

Mentor's mission

This section provides an overview of the roles that a mentor plays during a relationship. It begins with a description of the four main mentoring stages. These stages exist in all mentoring relationships. A mentor can begin a relationship at any of these stages after determining the mentee's level of experience and basic needs. It is most common, however, to start with the first of the four stages described here. How long each stage lasts will be different for every mentoring relationship. It is part of the mentor's and mentee's skills and judgment to recognize when the relationship has come to the end of a phase and it is time to move on. Typically, in most relationships, one phase overlaps another to a certain extent.

1

DEPENDENCY

WHAT IT IS

The word “dependency” can have negative associations of over-reliance, but in this context it merely is a way of describing how the mentoring relationship usually begins. The protégé, through the mere fact of being the younger and more inexperienced partner who is seeking help, will be more dependent on the older and wiser individual, which is not to say the mentee won’t be taking initiatives or learning lessons quickly. The mentor’s goal will be to ensure that this dependency decreases over a period of time until the mentee has reached “maturity” and is no longer dependent, at all, on the mentor.

WHAT HAPPENS

The mentor tries to pin down the protégé’s main career concerns and goals. Both are also learning to understand each other’s expectations. This is the period when the mentor will spend longer, more concentrated periods with the mentee, trying to build up his or her self-confidence through attention and praise. The mentor will also be throwing at the mentee the greatest amount of information, as well as sharing past experiences.

Mentor's mission continued

2 DEVELOPMENT

WHAT IT IS
Development refers basically to the protégé's developing skills.

WHAT HAPPENS
Having built the mentee's confidence, the mentor can now encourage him or her, under close supervision, to

- Branch out more on his or her own
- Ask more questions
- Seek new experiences

Communication between the two sides is already more balanced and equal.

3 FLIGHT

WHAT IT IS

Flight suggests the candidate can take off in various directions almost completely independently.

WHAT HAPPENS

The protégé is now able to embark on his or her own projects, with the mentor acting mainly as a sounding board. Apart from encouragement, all other interference is minimal.

4 INDEPENDENCE

WHAT IT IS

The mentee is ready to end the relationship, hopefully in a positive way.

WHAT HAPPENS

The mentee is ready to confront new challenges, completely on his or her own. The mentee may even be ready to start mentoring less experienced individuals.

Mentor roles

There are many roles a mentor has to assume depending on the needs of the protégé. Often, a mentor may have to perform several roles at once.

This next section outlines the characteristics and main functions of four of the principal and most common mentor roles.

1 TEACHER

WHEN DO YOU PERFORM?

The role of teacher is far more prevalent during the "dependency" period as this is the time when a protégé is spending the most time amassing new skills.

2 SPONSOR

WHEN DO YOU PERFORM?

As a sponsor, you are typically creating opportunities for the mentee or opening doors for him or her through suggestions and referrals. Because these are specific tasks, they are likely to be performed during the development or flight stage, only after the relationship has been established and several career goals have been set.

3

COUNSELOR

WHEN DO YOU PERFORM?

Like teaching, listening to the mentee's needs is going to be crucial in the early, dependency stages although if the relationship is trusting and open, your role as listener will continue at later stages but with less intensity. As mentor, a key part of your role is to enable the mentee to draw on inherent skills and realize that he or she has the abilities to fulfill new roles. Listening as he or she works through situations and scenarios with you, and reaches personal conclusions on the way forward, is important for the mentee's development. You are acting in many ways as a sounding board for his or her ideas.

4

CAREER ADVISOR

WHEN DO YOU PERFORM?

Your role as career advisor is key to being a mentor, and you will be tackling the mentee's career goals from the outset. Being up to speed on potential career paths that the mentee could follow is important to the success of the relationship.

Mentor as teacher

1

REVIEW JOB DESCRIPTION

You need to find out what the mentee's current job is and write down a list of the basic requirements. Do the same with any future job to which the candidate aspires.

2

PROVIDE DIRECTION

You are not literally required to be a teacher or have knowledge of all the areas the protégé needs to have. You do need to know, however, how to point him or her in the right direction. You might know senior colleagues who are experts in the particular field or know what courses, seminars, and conferences will prove useful.

3

SHARE EXPERIENCE

Because a mentor is not prescribing a way of working but rather helping the mentee find out ways to proceed, you provide a very useful service by sharing your experience with similar challenges. You might point out some of the mistakes you made and how you were able to turn them into positive experiences. Show the mentee that making mistakes is part of the learning process.

4

TEST SKILLS

You need to know how well the protégé can fulfill his or her job. You might test the mentee by assigning a specific task that is related to the current job.

- Does the mentee already possess all the necessary skills?
- Are they transferable to a future job that the mentee is interested in?
- Do goals require more knowledge, perhaps a foreign language?

5

PROVIDE INSIDER TIPS

Much valuable information on the workings of companies and businesses cannot be learned in books or courses. This is particularly the case with the dynamics of office politics, which can present many inexperienced people with new challenges.

6

GIVE FEEDBACK

Providing feedback is crucial. Feedback should be positive, regular, and specific. Make sure any criticism is of behavior, not the person.

Mentor as sponsor

1

FILL THE MISSING LINKS

Once the mentee knows broadly what he or she is striving for and identified what skills or work experience are needed to achieve these goals, the mentor can help the mentee create a plan of attack to fill these missing links. For instance, if a mentee discovers that he needs to complete an MBA to supplement his experience, the mentor can help him choose an MBA program by suggesting he call any contacts that have direct experience with MBAs. Alternatively, a protégé may have completed an MBA but still lack crucial work experience and the mentor can refer him to certain companies he knows of that are interested in MBA graduates.

2

PROVIDE CONTACTS

Knowing the right people to talk to is one of the most valuable assets for a mentee. With your considerable experience, you as mentor are likely to have a good contacts book so that you can target a list of three to five people who will be most useful to the mentee. You may offer to call the contact beforehand or just pass on numbers. In both cases, most of the effort and work should come from the mentee. You as mentor are the facilitator, not the doer.

3

RECOMMEND ACTIVITIES

Sometimes, the only way to learn about a new line of work is actually to experience it. For younger candidates, an internship may prove the most viable approach because it is otherwise difficult to get short-term experience in a company. As mentor you can recommend a placement at a company you know about. If you and the mentee are based in the same company, you may suggest additional tasks at work that are not in the mentee's everyday job description but that he or she will look at and provide feedback on. It's important that the mentee is fully prepared for the challenge. If the task is too difficult for the mentee, the experience will discourage further initiatives.

4

SHARE YOUR WORKING DAY

Assuming that you as mentor are still in full-time or even part-time work, you can invite the mentee to shadow you for a day or longer so the mentee can observe a new type of activity. Bring the mentee along to your meetings and workgroups. By following you, the protégé can also observe how you interact with others and how you handle situations. In these situations, your role as sponsor is supplemented with your function as a "role model."

Mentor as counselor

1

LISTEN

This sounds very easy but actually to be an effective listener requires many skills:

- You have to remain nonjudgmental, accepting the protégé's values and opinions without imposing your own.
- You have to make the mentee feel comfortable about opening up about his or her problems and aspirations. Try questions like: "Could you be more specific as to why you feel this way?" or "Why don't you explain to me how it started" or "How often do you feel that way?"
- You have to be comfortable with silences. For example, if you talk too soon, the mentee is likely to break up his train of thought, especially in the earlier stages when he is more nervous. Let him express himself at his own pace.
- Don't respond critically to any emotional outbursts. The mentee shouldn't feel ashamed or guilty about any loss of composure.

- Concentrate. If you feel your mind wandering, try to think about the main ideas, focus on the mentee's facial expressions, and ignore the surroundings.

- Don't allow any note-taking to interfere with listening. It is better to listen; then make notes to summarize key points toward the end of the meeting.

- Be aware of the importance of nonverbal signs. These include appropriate eye contact. Don't let your eyes wander about when the person is telling you something important. If the person breaks down, however, don't stare intensely. Show that you are understanding certain points by nodding or smiling. Try to keep your arms at your sides and not crossed, which may suggest that you are on the defensive. Similarly, sit comfortably, but sit upright so that it is clear that you are being businesslike.

Mentor as counselor continued

2

DON'T DIAGNOSE

It is difficult not to step in and give an opinion on what is going wrong with a mentee's performance and attitude, particularly in the early stages of the relationship when the protégé is typically most confused and in need of direction. However, you must avoid this temptation and remember that you are not assuming the role of a psychoanalyst even if you are performing some of his functions. The mentee has to diagnose what is lacking in his or her performance and work with you to put it right.

3

SHARPEN MENTEE'S PROBLEM-SOLVING SKILLS

People learn valuable lessons best when they work things out for themselves. Encourage this process by asking the mentee to write down at least three reasons why something isn't working and to list the pros and cons of each reason to evaluate which one best describes the situation. Even if you have a personal opinion, keep it to yourself. Keep asking open-ended questions that force the mentee to constantly reassess the situation and to explore the different alternatives. Open-ended questions generally start with "How," "Why," "What," or a similar interrogative, and do not invite a simple "yes" or "no" answer.

Mentor as career advisor

1

DETERMINE INTERESTS

It's not easy for many people, especially as they are starting a career, to have defined long-term career goals. To help them out, start off by defining some of their interests. Ask questions like:

- What aspects of your current job do you most like?
- What activities do you enjoy outside the office? If your mentee is still having trouble coming up with specific interests, get them to rank their interests in four broad areas such as: working with people; doing research; working with numbers; dealing with planning and strategic thinking.

2

ASSESS SKILLS

Like a teacher, you need to find out what skills the candidate has to promote. Like the set of interests, people find it difficult to analyze their own skills for several reasons:

- The have a sense of modesty.
- They discount skills acquired in earlier jobs or skills acquired outside the workplace.
- They forget other skills they learned but don't actually practice at present.

Tell them to note down any skill they have used in the last five years, no matter how trivial.

Mentor as career advisor continued

3

SPECIFY JOB ACCOMPLISHMENTS

When people have been doing a job for some time, they may forget about some key achievements because these have become incorporated into their pattern of everyday work and no longer appear significant. Ask leading questions like:

- What are your three biggest accomplishments in the last six months?
- What skills and abilities did you have to show to meet these responsibilities?
- What is your major achievement in your career so far?

4

IDENTIFY TASKS

By discussing goals and what needs to be done to reach that objective, the mentee now has a much clearer idea of what skills he or she already has to help get to that future point and what areas of expertise he or she is still missing and what can be done to fill these gaps.

5 IDENTIFY GOALS

Now that you've made the mentee think more carefully about his or her interests and skills, it is easier for the mentee to define wider questions about mid- to long-term career goals that may not be linked necessarily to their current job. Ask questions like:

- Where do you see yourself in five years?
- Do you know what you will have to accomplish to reach these goals?
- Do you know other people who have had these goals and achieved them?

6 MONITOR DEVELOPMENT

It's useful to review career goals with the mentee every three to six months to evaluate progress and check that his goals and objectives have not changed.

Evaluating the relationship

It is important for both mentor and mentee to evaluate the mentoring relationship, whether expectations are being met or exceeded, and if both parties are satisfied. If either side is finding it difficult to pin down exactly why a relationship may not be working successfully, these are some key questions that both mentor and mentee should answer honestly.

1

IS THERE RESPECT?

You can't expect to enjoy mutual respect from the outset of a relationship but if respect doesn't increase over time, then there are few chances of success. At the outset, the greater respect is likely to come from the mentee who has specifically chosen the mentor for the skills, knowledge, and abilities he or she would like to have. By demonstrating the will to succeed and the ability to take on board advice from the mentor, the mentee can also gain respect from the mentor.

2

IS THERE TRUST?

Trust is essential to a mentoring relationship. To achieve trust, there has to be open communication. The mentor should feel free to challenge the mentee without facing hostility, and the mentee has to be ready to ask a lot of questions without feeling he or she is being judged or criticized. Both parties must be honest from the start about what they want to achieve.

3

IS THERE LOYALTY?

When a mentor is in the same company as the mentee, it is vital that the protégée knows that whatever he or she says about the present job and the company will remain confidential from other bosses or directors. A mentor should remain loyal to this and not discuss the mentee's problems with others, even outside the company. Conversely, the mentee should not talk about any anecdotes about former jobs that the mentor has related in private.

Evaluating the relationship continued

4

IS THERE A PARTNERSHIP?

Ultimately, the mentee is building up his or her own career and must do this as an individual, but while he or she is striving for it, there need to be elements of a partnership in the relationship. The mentor must show excitement for the mentee's achievements and feel some involvement with the process while not unduly influencing the final result. The mentee can nurture this feeling of partnership by sharing information about key developments and setbacks.

5

HAS THE MENTEE BUILT SELF-ESTEEM?

It's inevitable that most mentees, even the most confident, have some issues regarding self-esteem, which is why they are seeking advice from a more experienced mentor. A mentor has fulfilled his role if at the end of the relationship, the mentee believes that he or she is a considerably more valued individual. The mentor should provide honest feedback and encourage the mentee to develop any skills that will help the mentee to do his or her job more efficiently and, as a result, feel better about him- or herself.

Ending the relationship

THE IDEAL ENDING

In the best-case scenarios, you know a mentoring relationship has reached a logical end when:

1 The protégé has reached full maturity to the point that he or she no longer requires the guidance of a mentor. A typical reaction is: "I had reached a point where I was fully conscious of my responsibilities and the steps I had to take in my career. I had outgrown the relationship."

2 The mentor and mentee wind down the frequency of their meetings. This doesn't mean that they don't meet for the occasional lunch or coffee, merely that the relationship is less intense, particularly from the point of view of the protégé who has, hopefully, achieved many of the goals that he or she outlined at the start of the process. The mentor too may be aware that he has outlasted his usefulness and if he has enjoyed the process, he may want to repeat the experience with another protégé.

LESS IDEAL ENDINGS

However, mentoring relationships also end for less positive reasons. It is useful to know about these to avoid them, either in present mentoring relationships or in future ones.

1 LOPSIDED MENTORING

This happens when either a mentor or mentee is spending far more energy and time on the relationship than the other. If this scenario arises, either party should be honest with the other and point this imbalance out. Perhaps the busy partner has been unaware of it or can offer a proper explanation for neglecting the relationship. They may have to spell out their time commitments to each other and explain how these may have changed since they first agreed to proceed with the mentoring relationship. This is why drawing up a contract, however informally, is a sensible idea. Sometimes, people have unrealistic expectations of what another person can do. Always allow a reasonable period of time for the busy partner to rectify the lopsided nature of the relationship. However, if there is little progress, then it is time to end the relationship.

Ending the relationship continued

2

CLASH OF PERSONALITIES

Sometimes, it doesn't matter how much goodwill existed at the outset, mentor and mentee possess clashing personalities and ways of working that only come to the fore when the relationship is in full swing. Opposing ways of doing things can be beneficial and a relationship where there are constant challenges and disagreements can have positive results. But when a nit-picker can no longer work in a partnership with a "big ideas" person who isn't interested in details, both parties must be honest and mature and decide that the relationship has outlasted its usefulness. After all, the relationship is mainly voluntary, and relations shouldn't feel forced.

3

CLASH WITH MENTEE'S BOSS

This scenario is more common when the mentor works in the same company as the mentee but is not the mentee's boss. The protégé's direct supervisor may be resentful of the relationship, believing that her authority is being undermined. To avoid this, the mentee should update his boss about parts of the mentoring relationship that are relevant to his job. He shouldn't allow any advice about his ultimate career plans to interfere negatively.

4

ULTERIOR MOTIVES

When mentor and mentee enter a relationship with ulterior motives that are not directly associated with mentoring, then the relationship is being built on a misconception. A mentor may believe it gives him prestige to have a protégé and spend too much time considering his own personal gain when the onus should be on the mentee. The mentee too may have chosen a mentor for his name and reputation without wanting to go through the sometimes difficult phases of being a mentee. If either side is suspicious of a hidden agenda, that party should try and bring it up tactfully. Avoid any direct accusations. Try instead asking open-ended questions like "Are you satisfied with the way the relationship is developing? Is it meeting your expectations?"

Ending the relationship continued

5

MISGUIDED EXPECTATIONS

Both mentor and mentee can fall into a trap of expecting too much from the other party. For instance, an experienced, senior director may expect a mentee to make far quicker progress than he is doing. She may think the slow progress reflects badly on her. A mentee, on the other hand, may be expecting the more experienced partner to work miracles and provide a fast track route to advancement. A written statement of intent at the outset of the relationship helps to iron out some of these confusions.

6

MENTOR'S JEALOUSY

There are occasions when the mentor can become jealous of the mentee's professional growth, especially if this means that the mentee no longer elicits or values the mentor's input or, in more extreme cases, starts bidding for work that the mentor may want.

7

COLLEAGUES' JEALOUSY

When the mentor works in the same company as the mentee, colleagues of the protégé who do not have a mentor may be resentful of the attention received by the mentee and the perceived route to advancement that will result from it. They can also accuse the mentor of favoritism to the mentee, even though they don't understand that they too have a right to ask a senior director to become a mentor. This is less of a problem in companies that have formal mentoring schemes in place, where there is greater transparency in the relationship.

8

PROFESSIONAL BOUNDARIES

The most classical example of a mentoring relationship becoming too personal is when either the mentor or mentee is keen for the relationship to become more personal. This tendency is particularly harmful for the mentor who can be accused of exploiting seniority and greater experience.

Conclusion

Coaching and mentoring have become management buzzwords, but neither practice is new. There is a tendency for the terms to be used interchangeably, and this book was conceived with the goal of setting the record straight, and positioning them as separate practices that yield different results. The material in Chapter 1 serves as a ready reminder of what each practice is (and is not), and who is likely to be involved in giving and receiving.

Although many individuals and most organizations understand their value, it is often the case that obstacles exist to coaching and mentoring. Chapter 2's exploration of what these might be allows you to focus on your own organization and understand, and remove, some of the constraints.

The material in Chapters 3 and 4, highlighting the benefits of coaching and mentoring for managers and subordinates, demonstrates that both practices yield positive results all around.

To enable executives to decide which practice (or indeed whether both) might meet their current needs, Chapters 5 and 6 show how they might work in practice.

From their first management position to their last, all executives benefit from coaching. And, as they gain more experience, most executives develop the coaching skills to pass on what they have learned to more junior staff. A manager whose own skills are first rate, can ensure that all his team members benefit. The material outlined in Chapter 5 is designed to help executives at all levels to evaluate their skills, identify gaps, and work toward filling them.

Mentoring is one of the most effective ways that senior personnel can give something back to the business or profession that has given them so much. As a mentor, you may find you reap enormous personal rewards, but mentoring is first and foremost an altruistic act on your part. If you have shied away from taking on this role, the insights into how the process might work for you, and where your potential mentee is coming from in terms of goals and expectations, outlined in Chapter 6, hopefully will help you to reevaluate your reluctance, and take on this valuable role.

Coaching and mentoring are both about helping people reach their full potential. A coach has an agenda to teach or reinforce skills; a mentor allows a mentee to develop his or her own skills. In the modern business world, both contribute to personal growth and professional success.

Index